Philosophy and
Real Politics

Raymond Geuss
Philosophy and Real Politics

PRINCETON UNIVERSITY PRESS

Princeton and Oxford

Copyright © 2008 by Princeton University Press

Published by Princeton University Press, 41 William Street, Princeton,

New Jersey 08540

In the United Kingdom: Princeton University Press,

99 Banbury Road, Oxford OX2 6JX

All Rights Reserved

First paperback printing, 2024

Paperback ISBN 978-0-691-25869-0

The Library of Congress has cataloged the cloth edition as follows:

Geuss, Raymond.

    Philosophy and real politics / Raymond Geuss.

    p. cm.

    Includes bibliographical references and index.

    ISBN 978-0-691-13788-9 (hardcover)   1. Political science—

Philosophy.   I. Title.

    JA71.G46 2008

    320.0—dc22   2007052740

British Library Cataloging-in-Publication Data is available

This book has been composed in Minion with Syntax display

Cover image provided by the estate of photographer John Sadovy /

www.JohnSadovy.com

press.princeton.edu

Contents

Preface   *vii*

Introduction   *1*

Part I   **Realism**

Who Whom?   *23*

Priorities, Preferences, Timing   *30*

Legitimacy   *34*

Tasks of Political Theory   *37*

    Understanding, Evaluation, Orientation   37

    Conceptual Innovation   42

    Ideology   50

Part II   **Failures of Realism**

Rights   *60*

Justice   *70*

Equality   *76*

Fairness, Ignorance, Impartiality   *80*

Power   *90*

Conclusion   *95*

Notes   *103*

Works Cited   *109*

Index   *113*

Preface

The following text is an expansion of a lecture I gave at the University of Athens in April 2007 under the title "(Lenin), Rawls, and Political Philosophy." The original lecture has since appeared in the journal *Cogito*, in a translation into Modern Greek, for which I wish to thank Dr. Vasso Kindi. My thanks also to Katerina Ierodiakonou for the kind invitation to speak in Athens. The death of my friend Michael Frede while swimming in the Gulf of Korinth in August 2007 prevents me from thanking him for three decades of hospitality and illuminating conversation, and specifically for the strong encouragement he gave me to publish the lecture. A mainstay of my intellectual life during the past year and a half has been the fortnightly German-language *Philosophisches Forschungskolloquium* based in the Cambridge Faculty of Philosophy; I have had the great good fortune to be able to discuss most of the material in this text extensively (in one form or another) with the members of that group: Manuel Dries, Fabian Freyenhagen, Richard Raatzsch, Jörg Schaub, and Christian Skirke. My thanks also to Rüdiger Bittner, John Dunn, Zeev Emmerich, Peter Garnsey, Istvan Hont, Quentin Skinner, and Ursula Wolf for discussions of the issues treated here and comments on the draft of this text. Needless to say, none of these individuals should be construed as necessarily agreeing with any particular claim I make in the text. I owe my greatest debt of gratitude to Hilary Gaskin for acute comments that have improved virtually every page of the manuscript. Ian Malcolm of the Princeton University Press has, as usual, been an unfailing source of sound advice, and a pleasure to work with.

Philosophy and
Real Politics

A strong "Kantian" strand is visible in much contemporary political theory, and even perhaps in some real political practice. This strand expresses itself in the highly moralised tone in which some public diplomacy is conducted, at any rate in the English-speaking world, and also in the popularity among political philosophers of the slogan "Politics is applied ethics." Slogans like this can be dangerous precisely because they are slickly ambiguous, and this one admits of at least two drastically divergent interpretations. There is what I will call "the anodyne" reading of the slogan, which formulates a view I fully accept, and then there is what I will call the "ethics-first" reading.

The anodyne reading asserts that "politics"—meaning both forms of political action and ways of studying forms of political action—is not and cannot be a strictly value-free enterprise, and so is in the very general sense an "ethical" activity. Politics is a matter of human, and not merely mechanical, interaction between individuals, institutions, or groups. It can happen that a group of passengers in an airplane are thrown together mechanically when it crashes, or that a man slipping off a bridge accidentally lands on a tramp sleeping under the bridge. The second of these two examples is a salutary reminder of the role of contingency and of the unexpected in history, but neither of the two cases is a paradigm for politics. Political actors are generally pursuing certain conceptions of the "good," and acting in the light of what they take to be permissible. This is true despite the undeniable fact that most human agents most of the time are weak, easily distracted, deeply conflicted, and confused, and that they therefore do not always do only things they take to be permissible. One will never understand what they are doing unless and until one takes seriously the ethical dimension of their action in the broadest sense of that term: their various value-judgments about the good, the permissible, the attractive, the preferable, that which is to be avoided at all costs. Acting in this way can perfectly reasonably be described as "applying ethics," provided one understands that "applying" has very few similarities with giving a proof in Euclidean geometry or calculating the load-bearing capacities of a bridge, and is often more like the process of trying to survive in a free-for-all. Provided also one keeps in mind a number of other important facts, such as the unavoidable indeterminacy of much of human life. Every point in a Cartesian coordinate system is construed as having a determinate distance from the x-axis and from the y-axis. This way of thinking is of extremely limited usefulness when one is dealing with any phenomenon connected with human desires, beliefs, attitudes, or values. People often have no determinate beliefs at all about a variety of subjects; they often don't know what they want or why they did something; even when they know or claim to know what they want, they can often give no coherent account of why exactly they want what they claim to want; they often have no idea which portions of their systems of beliefs and desires—to the extent to which they have determinate beliefs and desires—are "ethical principles" and which are (mere empirical) "interests." This is not simply an epistemic failing, and also not something that one could in principle remedy, but a pervasive "inherent" feature in human life. Although this fundamental indeterminacy is a phenomenon almost everyone confronts and recognises in his or her own case all the time, for a variety of reasons we are remarkably resistant to accepting it as a general feature of the way in which we should best think about our social life, but we are wrong to try to evade it. A further reason to be suspicious of quasi-Cartesian attitudes to human life is that people are rarely more than locally consistent in action, thought, and desire, and in many domains of human life this does not matter at all, or might even be taken to have positive value. I may pursue a policy that is beneficial to me in the short term, but that "in the long run" will undermine itself. This may not even be subjectively "irrational," given that in the *long* run, as Keynes pointed out, I will be dead (along with all the rest of us), and I may very reasonably, or even correctly, believe that I will be lucky enough to die before the policy unravels. When Catullus expresses his love *and* hate for Lesbia, he is not obviously voicing a wish to rid himself of one or the other of these two sentiments. Not all contradictions resolve into temporal change of belief or desire. Any attempt to think seriously about the relation between politics and ethics must remain cognitively sensitive to the fact that people's beliefs, values, desires, moral conceptions, etc., are usually half-baked (in every sense), are almost certain to be both indeterminate and, to the extent to which they are determinate, grossly inconsistent in any but the most local, highly formalised contexts, and are constantly changing.[1] None of this implies that it might not be of the utmost importance to aspire to ensure relative stability and consistency in certain limited domains.

Humans' beliefs and desires are in constant flux, and changes in them can take place for any number of reasons. Transformations of specific sectors of human knowledge are often accompanied by very widespread further changes in worldview and values. People have often claimed that Darwinism had this effect in Europe at the end of the nineteenth century. In addition, new technologies give people new possible objects of desire and, arguably, new ways of desiring things. It is by no means obvious that the hunger which was satisfied when Neolithic humans tore apart raw meat with their fingers is the same kind of thing as the hunger that is satisfied by dining in a five-star restaurant in 2008.[2] Technological change can also make it possible for people to act in new ways toward each other, and sometimes these need to be regulated in ways for which there are no precedents: once it begins to become possible to transfer human organs from one person to another, and manipulate the genetic makeup of the members of the next generation of humans, people come to feel the need of some kind of guidance about which forms of transfer or manipulation should be permitted and which discouraged or forbidden. Changes in political or economic power relations often make it more or less likely that certain groups will move culturally closer to or further away from their neighbours, thus changing people's ethical concepts, sentiments, and views (again, in the broadest sense of the term "ethical"). Politics is in part informed by and in part an attempt to manage some of these changes. In addition, as people act on their values, moral views, and conceptions of the good life, these values and conceptions often *change* precisely as the result of being "put into practice." Sometimes one could describe this as a kind of "learning" experience. The total failure of a project that has absorbed a significant amount of social energy and attention, and for which serious sacrifices have been made, in particular often seems to focus the mind and make it open to assimilating new ways of thinking and valuing.[3] Thus after the events of 1914 to 1945 a very significant part of the population in Germany became highly sceptical of nationalism and the military virtues, and the experiences of Suez and Algeria tended in Britain and France to throw any further attempts at acting out the old forms of colonial imperialism into disrepute. Sometimes, to be sure, the appropriate learning process does not take place, or the "wrong" lesson is drawn, and this often exacts a high price in the form of a repetition or failure. Thus the larger significance of the Reagan era in the United States was that the political class in power to a large extent prevented any significant, long-term lessons from being drawn from the defeat in Vietnam. Learning, failure to learn, and drawing the wrong lesson are all possible outcomes, and whichever one in fact results needs to be explained, understood, and evaluated. There is no guarantee that "learning" is irreversible, nor can any distinct sense be attributed to the claim that learning in the longer term is natural, that is, will take place *unless* prevented.[4] Furthermore, even in the best of cases learning in politics seems to be limited either to very crude transformations over long periods—"we learn" over two thousand years that it is better to have a legal code that is accessible to everyone than merely to allow the priests to consult their esoteric lore—or to what are, in historical terms, very short periods, with little in between. The effects of the short-term learning can often wear off remarkably quickly. Colonial intervention was in bad odour in Britain between the 1960s and the year 2000, but we now (2007) have troops fighting in Iraq and Afghanistan again.

One can speak of politics as "applied ethics" if this form of words takes one's fancy, but it is not obvious that all the above-described phenomena form anything like a natural kind or a single coherent domain for study by some determinate intellectual speciality: "applied ethics" is just a term applied to people trying to manage forms of action and modes of evaluation that distinguish a good from better or less good as they interact with political programmes, individual and group interests, changes in the economic structure, the requirements of action, institutional needs, and contingently arising historical problems of various kinds.

When I object to the claim that politics is applied ethics, I do not have the above anodyne reading in mind. Rather, I intend a much more specific view about the nature and structure of ethical judgment and its relation to politics, and in particular a theory about where one should *start* in studying politics, what the final framework for studying politics is, what it is reasonable to focus on, and what it is possible to abstract from. "Politics is applied ethics" in the sense I find objectionable means that we *start* thinking about the human social world by trying to get what is sometimes called an "ideal theory" of ethics. This approach assumes that there is, or could be, such a thing as a separate discipline called Ethics which has its own distinctive subject-matter and forms of argument, and which prescribes how humans should act toward one another. It further assumes that one can study this subject-matter without constantly locating it within the rest of human life, and without unceasingly reflecting on the relations one's claims have with history, sociology, ethnology, psychology, and economics. Finally, this approach proposes that the way to proceed in "ethics" is to focus on a very few general principles such as that humans are rational, or that they generally seek pleasure and try to avoid pain, or that they always pursue their own "interests"; these principles are taken to be historically invariant, and studying ethics consists essentially in formulating them clearly, investigating the relations that exist between them, perhaps trying to give some kind of "justification" of at least some of them, and drawing conclusions from them about how people ought to act or live. Usually, some kind of individualism is also presupposed, in that the precepts of ethics are thought to apply directly and in the first instance to human individuals. Often, although not invariably, views of this type also give special weight to "ethical intuitions" that people in our society purportedly share, and they hold that an important part of ethics is the attempt to render these intuitions consistent.

Empirical abstemiousness and systematicity are two of the major virtues to which "ideal" theories of this kind aspire. The best-known instance of this approach is Kantianism, which claims in its more extreme versions that ethics can be completely nonempirical, derived simply (but fully) from the mere notion of rational agency, and the absolute consistency of willing that is purportedly the defining characteristic of any rational agent. Kantian ethics is supposed to be completely universal in its application to all agents in all historical situations. Although Kant does not himself use the vocabulary of "intuitions" (or rather, he does use a term usually translated "intuition" (*Anschauung*), but uses it with no specific moral meaning), he does think that individuals have in common sense ("der gemeine Menschenverstand")[5]— presumably post-Christian, Western European common sense—a reliable "compass" that tells them what they ought to do in individual cases. Philosophical ethics does nothing more than formulate the principle that such common sense in fact uses. Kantianism is at the moment the most influential kind of "ideal" theory, but one can find similar structural features in many other views (e.g., in some forms of utilitarianism), and they are the more pronounced, the keener their proponents are to proclaim the strictly "philosophical" nature of the kind of study of ethics that they advocate. A theory of this kind might consist of constraints on action, such as the "Thou shalt not kill; thou shalt not steal" of various archaic moral codes or Kant's "Never lie even to save a human life"; or it might also contain the presentation of some ideal goals to be pursued, such as "Strive to construct (an ideal) democracy" (or "Strive to construct an ideal speech community," or "Strive to build socialism") or "Love thy neighbour as thyself." The view I am rejecting assumes that one can complete the work of ethics first, attaining an ideal theory of how we should act, and then in a second step, one can apply that ideal theory to the action of political agents. As an observer of politics one can morally judge the actors by reference to what this theory dictates they ought to have done. Proponents of the view I am rejecting then often go on to make a final claim that a "good" political actor should guide his or her behaviour by applying the ideal theory. The empirical details of the given historical situation enter into consideration only at this point. "Pure" ethics as an ideal theory comes first, then applied ethics, and politics is a kind of applied ethics.

In this essay I would like to expound and advocate a kind of political philosophy based on assumptions that are the opposite of the "ethics-first" view, and so it might be useful to the reader to make the acquaintance, in a preliminary and sketchy way, of the four interrelated theses that, I will claim, ought to structure a more fruitful approach to politics than "ethics-first."

First, political philosophy must be realist. That means, roughly speaking, that it must start from and be concerned in the first instance not with how people ought ideally (or ought "rationally") to act, what they ought to desire, or value, the kind of people they ought to be, etc., but, rather, with the way the social, economic, political, etc., institutions actually operate in some society at some given time, and what really does move human beings to act in given circumstances. The emphasis on *real motivation* does not require that one deny that humans have an imaginative life that is important to them, aspirations, ideals they wish to pursue, or even moral views that influence their behaviour. It also does not imply that humans are not sometimes "rational," or that it would not often be of great benefit to them to be "rational." What it does mean, to put it tautologically, is that these ideals and aspirations influence their behaviour and hence are politically relevant, only to the extent to which they do actually influence behaviour in some way. Just because certain ideal or moral principles "look good" or "seem plausible" to us, to those who propose them or to those to whom they are proposed—to the prophet or to the people whom the prophet addresses—it does not follow that these norms, canons, or principles will have any particular effect at all on how people will really act. Even if one were to assume something I am loath to admit, namely, that certain moral principles that have *determinate content*[6] are "absolutely true" or "eternally valid" or could be "ultimately justified by reference to the nature of reason itself," this would not automatically ensure that these principles were in fact universally recognised— what truths except utterly trivial and banal ones are "universally" recognised? It would also not ensure that, even if they were recognised, they would be universally obeyed. Finally, a political philosopher cannot take ideals, models for behaviour, or utopian conceptions at their own face value. That the prophet claims and genuinely believes that his table of values will bring peace and prosperity to his followers, and even that the followers genuinely believe this and act according to the table of values to the best of their ability, does not ensure that peace and prosperity will in fact follow. Even if the population did prosper, that would not, in itself, show that the prophet had been right. This could just have been luck, or the result of completely different factors. A realist can fully admit that products of the human imagination are very important in human life, provided he or she keeps a keen and unwavering eye upon the basic motto *Respice finem*, meaning in this case not "The best way to live is to keep your mind on your end: death," but "Don't look just at what they say, think, believe, but at what they actually do, and what *actually happens* as a result." An imagined threat might be an extremely powerful motivation to action, and an aspiration, even if built on fantasy, is not nothing, provided it really moves people to action. This does not mean that it is any less important to distinguish between a correct perception of the world and illusion. The opposite of reality or the correct perception of reality is in any case not the imagination but illusion; however, even illusions can have effects. The realist must take powerful illusions seriously as factors in the world that have whatever motivational power they in fact have for the population in question, that is, as something to be understood. This is compatible with seeing through them, and refusing steadfastly to make them part of the cognitive apparatus one employs oneself to try to make sense of the world. It is no sign of gimlet-eyed realism to deny the enormous real significance of religious practices, beliefs, and institutions in the world, past and present, but, rather, a sign of simple blindness. This, however, does not imply that the cognitive or normative claims made by religious believers have any plausibility whatever.

Second, and following on from this, political philosophy must recognise that politics is in the first instance about action and the contexts of action,[7] not about mere beliefs or propositions. In many situations agents' beliefs can be very important—for instance, knowing what another agent believes is often a relevant bit of information if one wants to anticipate how that agent can be expected to act—but sometimes agents do not immediately act on beliefs they hold. In either case the study of politics is primarily the study of actions and only secondarily of beliefs that might be in one way or another connected to action. To reiterate, propounding a theory, introducing a concept, passing on a piece of information, even, sometimes, entertaining a possibility, are all actions, and as such they have preconditions and consequences that must be taken into account. When at the Potsdam Conference in 1945 Truman told Stalin about the successful explosion of the first atomic bomb, this was not merely an exchange of a bit of information about the results of a physical experiment that had succeeded; rather, in doing this Truman was also performing a certain action, one of trying to intimidate Stalin, to discourage him from acting in certain ways, etc. In fact that was the *point* of Truman's action, and, whether one is Stalin or a student of twentieth-century history, one fails to understand the action at all if one fails to take that point. Even general doctrines or complex theories can have distinct effects not merely on particular courses of action, but on the general structure of action in a given society. If utilitarian philosophy, Roman law, Darwinism, Chicago-style neoliberal economics, or "rational decision theory" is taught in *all* the schools, this will probably, to some extent, influence the way agents in the society come to act. This does not mean that we, or anyone, know what the nature of that influence will be. It certainly does not mean that if all schoolchildren are taught "rational decision theory" they will all *become* fully "rational agents" (in the sense specified by the theory) even if they try hard to do so, because the actual consequence might be, for instance, that *some* become more like the purely rational choosers described in the theory than they would otherwise have been, but others find themselves rebelling. Dostoyevski's Underground Man decides he would rather be anything than a piano key or an organ stop.[8] There is nothing unreasonable about not wanting to be fully "rational" if "rationality" is understood in a sufficiently narrow way. Paul of Tarsus at the beginning of Christianity notably describes the Christian faith as "folly" (μωρία), but this did not prevent it from informing European sensibilities for a rather long period of time. Six years of constant religious instruction does not ensure religious belief, and six years of public repetition of the demands of elementary hygiene won't make quite every person in the country brush his (or her) teeth after every meal. Still, when the Medical Council issues a warning about the dangers of smoking, this is not merely the enunciation of a scientific result, which can be evaluated according to the usual canons of empirical support, but *also* an intervention that will have effects, one way or the other, on social and political life. The only way to tell what effects there will be is to study them. There is, of course, nothing inherently absurd in holding that when Truman told Stalin that an atomic bomb had been successfully tested, one could make this event an object of two complementary, but distinct enquiries. First, one could study this as an action that will have, and was intended to have, various consequences, and which can be evaluated in various ways, e.g., as appropriate or not, prudent or not, etc.; or, second, one could investigate the content of the claim—that the test had been successful—as something that was warranted (or not) by available evidence.

The third thesis I want to defend is that politics is historically located: it has to do with humans interacting in institutional contexts that change over time, and the study of politics must reflect this fact. This is not an objection to generalising; we don't even know what it would be like to think without generalising. Nevertheless, it simply turns out as a matter of fact that excessive generalising ends up not being informative. There are no interesting "eternal questions" of political philosophy. It is perfectly true that if one wishes, one can construct some universal empirical truths about human beings and the societies they form, e.g., it is correct that people in general try to keep themselves alive and that all humans have had to eat to survive, and that this has imposed various constraints on the kind of human societies that have been possible, but such statements, taken on their own, are not interestingly informative for the purposes of politics.[9] Such detached general statements do not wear their meaning on their sleeves; in fact, understanding politics means seeing that such statements have clear meaning at all only relative to their specific context, and this context is one of historically structured forms of action. For an isolated general statement like the one about the human need to eat to be enlightening, one must relate it to issues such as: what form of food production takes place in the society in question, who has control over it, what form that control takes, and what food taboos are observed.[10] If one takes such generalisations to be more than what they really are— mere schemata that need to be filled with concrete historical content—and uses them in isolation as part of an attempt to understand real politics, they will be seriously misleading. People do not eat "food in general" but rice, or wheaten bread, or shellfish, or pork, or they do *not* eat beef or pork or larvae, and people have sometimes willingly starved themselves to death. Suicide through self-starvation is perhaps an extreme case that needs special explanation (of a psychopathological kind, as in anorexia, or of an ideological kind, as with the Irish hunger strikers of the 1960s), but how is one to know beforehand that a given situation with which one is confronted is not extreme? If one wants understanding or any kind of guidance for action, one will have to take the specific cultural and historical circumstances into consideration. *What level* of historical specificity is required for what purpose is itself a question that has no general answer. Looking for a set of formulae that are as historically invariant as possible and assuming that those formulae will allow us to grasp what is most important will point one in the wrong direction. If one thinks that understanding one's world is a minimal precondition to having sensible human desires and projects, history is not going to be dispensable. The more important one thinks it is to act, the more this will be the case. For as long, at least, as human societies continue to change, we won't escape history.

Finally, the fourth assumption that lies behind this essay is that politics is more like the exercise of a craft or art, than like traditional conceptions of what happens when a theory is applied. It requires the deployment of skills and forms of judgment that cannot easily be imparted by simple speech, that cannot be reliably codified or routinised, and that do not come automatically with the mastery of certain theories. A skill is an ability to act in a flexible way that is responsive to features of the given environment with the result that action or interaction is enhanced or facilitated, or the environment is transformed in ways that are positively valued. Sometimes the result will be a distinct object or product: a shoe, a painting, a building, a boat; sometimes there will be no distinct object produced, as when a skilful marriage counsellor changes the interaction between spouses in a positive way or a vocal coach helps a singer bring out some rather subtle aspects of an overplayed aria. One of the signs that I have acquired a skill, rather than that I have been simply mechanically repeating things I have seen others do, have been applying a handbook, or have just been lucky, is that I can attain interesting and positively valued results in a variety of different and unexpected circumstances. A skilful painter can produce an appropriate image even using newly created materials that have never before been used for this purpose. To the extent to which the circumstances are genuinely different and unexpected, it is unlikely that there will be any already existing body of theoretical work that gives direct advice about how to deal with them, or models of the successful exercise of skill in those circumstances that could be emulated.

The attentive reader will notice that I use the terms "political theory" and "political philosophy" (the latter sometimes assumed to be more general than the former) almost interchangeably, and that I do not distinguish sharply between a descriptive theory and a "pure normative theory" (the former purportedly giving just the facts; the latter moral principles, imperatives, or ideal norms). This is fully intentional, and indeed part of the point I am trying to make. I want precisely to try to cast as much doubt as I can on the universal usefulness of making these distinctions. Kantians, of course, will think I have lost the plot from the start; and that only confusion can result from failure to make these essential, utterly fundamental divisions between Is and Ought, Fact and Value, or the Descriptive and the Normative in as rigorous and systematic a way as possible, just as I think they have fallen prey to a kind of fetishism, attributing to a set of human conceptual inventions a significance that they do not have. By doing this, in my view, they condemn themselves to certain forms of ignorance and illusion, and introduce into their cognitive and political practice a rigidity and deformation it need not have. Politics allows itself to be cut up for study in any one of a number of different ways, and which cuts will be most illuminating will depend very much on the context, on what one is interested in finding out. There is no single canonical style of theorising about politics. One can ask any number of perfectly legitimate questions about different political phenomena, and depending on the question, different kinds of enquiry will be appropriate. Asking what the question is, and why the question is asked, is always asking a pertinent question. In some contexts a *relative* distinction between "the facts" and human valuations of those facts (or "norms") might be perfectly useful, but the division makes sense only relative to the context, and can't be extracted from that context, promoted, and declared to have absolute standing. However, I also think that the most convincing way to make this point is not by a frontal attack on the Is/Ought distinction, which would be very tedious, given that I grant that one can make the distinction in virtually any *particular* context, as a relative distinction. The Is/ Ought distinction looks overwhelmingly plausible because of the way philosophers have traditionally framed the question and assumed one would have to go about answering it. It is the misleading focus on artificially simple, invented examples that seems to give the distinction its hold over us. So rather than talking at great length and to no clear purpose about the Is/Ought distinction in general, I would like to proceed indirectly by inviting the reader to see how much more interesting the political world seems to be, and how much more one can come to learn and understand about it, if one relaxes the straightjacket and simply ignores this purported distinction.

A book of this kind, and especially of this size, cannot possibly treat all, or even any, of the issues it raises in anything like a full and satisfactory way. It also cannot aspire to change the minds of people who already have firmly fixed settled opinions on how political philosophy "must" be done. Rather, the most it can hope to do is address people who have perhaps occasionally had similar thoughts already themselves or those whose views are for one reason or another unformed or unsettled. To them it wishes to suggest the possibility that there might be a viable way of thinking about politics that is orthogonal to the mainstream of contemporary analytic political philosophy.

Part I

Realism

Modern political philosophy begins in Europe in the seventeenth century when Hobbes attempts to find a solution to the problem his contemporaries have in living together without assuming either a divinely ordained and enforced order, or a naturally implanted, invariable, and irresistibly powerful human impulse toward one particular form of cooperative action. Any entity that modern political agents would recognise as a human being in the full sense has grown up as a member of a human group, that is, among other humans who interact with each other in a certain way, minimally in what is called a "nuclear family" and most likely in a family embedded in a variety of larger kinship groups, loose networks of friends and neighbours, and perhaps more formal political structures. Although, however, it seems a natural and not an artificial fact about humans as we know them—to the extent to which one can make this distinction at all—that we are in this sense social and not solitary creatures, it is also the case that in modern societies human interaction is not something that can ever be taken for granted; it is always potentially disrupted, unstable, and conflict-ridden. The members of a human group are not parts of a single organism, like the hands or feet of an animal, who have no will of their own, nor are we like bees, ants, or even herd animals whose strong natural instincts can be counted on, at least in some areas, to be powerful enough to assure more or less harmonious coordination. Rather, humans, even in the most repressive societies we know, grow up to be individuated creatures who are separate centres for the formation, evaluation, and revision of beliefs, attitudes, values, and desires, and for the initiation of action that puts these beliefs and desires into effect. So coordination of action in our societies, either of a negative kind (that I don't act so as to thwart your plans) or of a positive kind (that I act so as to maximise the attainment of some goal that can be reached only by joint effort) is always a social achievement, and it is something attained and preserved, and generally achieved only at a certain price. People are very quick to observe that there is a wide variety of different ways in which collective action can be organised, and, given that different forms of collective action are also differentially beneficial, this in itself may well motivate some to try to change existing patterns.

What I wish to call "the realist approach to political philosophy" develops this basically Hobbesian insight. It is centred on the study of historically instantiated forms of collective human action with special attention to the variety of ways in which people can structure and organise their action so as to limit and control forms of disorder that they might find excessive or intolerable for other reasons. This is a historically specific study if only because the concepts of "order" and "intolerable disorder" are themselves variable magnitudes. That is, people's general level of tolerance of unregimented, unpredictable, or random action, and the extent to which specific kinds of lack of order particularly trouble them, vary considerably from one time and one society to another. Thus few modern Western European populations would tolerate the anarchic freedom to own private firearms that is held to be a positive constituent of the good life in the United States, or the freedom from a nationally organized form of health insurance; and from the twelfth to the seventeenth century a society *not* based on religious uniformity was almost unthinkable. One person's disorder is sometimes another's freedom, and so much conceptual confusion reigns in this area that even Baghdad in 2003 could be described with a straight face by U.S. Secretary of Defense Donald Rumsfeld as an instance of "untidy freedom." The variation in the perception of what counts as "order" or "freedom" is often itself a source of tension between individuals and groups. One of two neighbouring countries can accept levels of petty border raiding as a natural concomitant of social life, while the other sees, or pretends to see, in it a casus belli.

The way to develop the realistic spirit of Hobbes in the contemporary world, I wish to suggest, is not by assuming that one needs an antecedent ontological specification of a distinct domain called "politics," but by considering a set of questions. When we speak of politics, we are generally thinking of possible answers to one or another, or several, of three kinds of question. For ease of reference I will call these the questions of Lenin, of Nietzsche, and of Max Weber. These questions will be rather loosely specified, and conjoining them means lumping together enquiries that actually differ in content and meaning, depending on the time at which they are posed, who is asking the question with what intention, who is being interrogated, and the purpose of the interrogation, but, then, that is precisely part of the point I wish to make.

Who Whom?

Lenin defines politics with characteristic clarity and pithiness when he says that it is concerned with the question that keeps recurring in our political life: "Who whom?" (кто кого) What this means in the first instance is that the impersonalised statements one might be inclined to make about human societies generally require, if they are to be politically informative, elaboration into statements about particular concrete people doing things to other people. The sign in the Underground that reads, "Non-payment of fare will be punished" means that a policeman may arrest and fine you, if you fail to buy a ticket; "Unemployment has risen by x percent" means that certain people who have control of particular economic organisations have done something concrete, terminated the employment, of certain other people.

To say that the question "Who whom?" "keeps recurring" does not, of course, mean that for literally every single human society that has existed or will exist this is a question that "necessarily" arises in every context. The extent to which it does arise, the forms in which it arises, and the importance of the question will vary historically. Perhaps there are contexts and societies in which this question is irrelevant, but for most of the societies with which we have direct dealings, and the ones to which we have relatively straightforward cognitive access, this is a question that arises again and again, and for what we can see are good reasons. One strand of "liberalism," represented, for instance, in the early writings of Humboldt,[11] is devoted to trying to imagine a structure of free political institutions, relative to which this question would be so unimportant that it would become irrelevant to ask who were the rulers and who were the ruled. The centrepiece of the argument was the idea of a strict limitation of government. *If* government was sufficiently limited, the thought ran, it would not matter who was in a position to operate the state apparatus, and who was subject to it. Utopian speculation, of course, is free and in some senses highly desirable, but if this liberal suggestion was intended to imply that such a free form of political organisation was actually *realisable* under nineteenth-, twentieth-, or twenty-first-century economic conditions, that was certainly an illusion.

Obviously, how specific the answer to the question "Who whom?" needs to be will depend on the time and place, and the purpose of the question. In some relatively simple cases and for some purposes the answer to the question might be the name of particular persons—Brian is Paul's line manager, so "Brian" is the "who" and Paul the "whom"—but in most cases in complex societies the answer will be the naming of an office, position, or institution. It is "a policeman"—whichever individual member of the police force is assigned that role—who arrests me for nonpayment of fare. That he happens to be PC John Jones is not relevant. How important it is to specify the individuals concerned, for instance designating them by their proper names, rather than simply referring to the roles or positions involved, will depend on the problem at issue and the kind of society in question. An important part of answering the question will be to discover what *kind* of answer is required in the specific circumstances, which is a question of proper categorisation.

Although Lenin's formula is basically correct, it is perhaps too dense and needs to be developed or extended: actually, I would argue, it needs to be extended twice. First of all, the formula should read not merely "Who whom?" but, rather, "Who <does> what to whom for whose benefit?" with four distinct variables to be filled in, i.e., (1) Who?, (2) What?, (3) To whom?, (4) For whose benefit? To think politically is to think about agency, power, and interests, and the relations among these. Who—which individuals or the bearers of which offices, positions, or roles—has control of employment in the society, and who have lost their jobs? Will those who have lost their jobs have access to alternative modes of subsistence or not? Who will provide those alternatives, and what exactly will they be (provision of cash payments, vouchers, or jobs in the public sector by the government, or of shelter and food by charities)? Are the unemployed organised, and capable of collective action, or are they disorganised and inert, and if they are organised, what form does this organisation take? What concretely has one party done to the other: How exactly will the policeman punish me? Will he give me a warning, impose a fine, hit me with his truncheon, or take me to jail? Will he also expect a bribe? Finally, who benefits and who does not from the transaction in question? Who derives distinct positive benefits from any individual action or type of action in a given society will often be an extremely complex question.

The second extension of Lenin's formula is connected with another important feature of our social life. We relate to other people not merely in terms of what they have done to us or are doing to us, but also with regard to what they will or *could* do to us. If I have certain effective powers, these may have a sufficiently intimidating effect on others that I get my way without ever needing actually to exercise these powers. So if we wish to understand how human action in a certain society comes to be coordinated, how some individuals or groups bring it about that others embark on certain courses of action or refrain from embarking on others, one of the things we will need to take into account is not just who actually does what to whom, but also who has what powers, i.e., who *could* do what to whom for whose benefit.

One must also take account not only of what powers an individual or group actually has, but also of how those powers are perceived, or not perceived, and what powers agents are, rightly or wrongly, *thought* to have by others (and by themselves). To think one has a power that one does not can give an agent self-confidence, which may be self-reinforcing (but also may not, depending on circumstances). Given the role that intimidation can play, one important "power" that an agent, whether an individual or a society, can have is the ability to control how others perceive its powers or what they *imagine* these powers to be.

In this account "power" is to be construed as connected with general concepts like "ability to do" (such as that I have the power of speech or of locomotion), rather than as designating exclusively a form of coercion (such as "the hostages remained in the power of the gang until they were freed by the police") or domination ("the Athenians reasserted their power over the island of Chios"). It is probably a mistake to treat "power" as if it referred to a single, uniform substance or relation wherever it was found. It makes more sense to distinguish a variety of qualitatively distinct kinds of powers. There are strictly coercive powers you may have by virtue of being physically stronger than me, persuasive powers by virtue of being convinced of the moral rightness of your case and having special training or a natural talent for speaking; you may be more powerful than I am by virtue of being a charismatic figure who is able to attract enthusiastic, voluntary support from others, or by virtue of being able to see and exploit a strategic, rhetorical, or diplomatic weakness in my position. Contemporary political scientists often contrast "hard" and "soft" power, and there is nothing wrong with this contrast provided one takes it as no more than a first, preliminary account of the different types and forms of power that one can discover in a given society. How many types one would have to distinguish would depend on the context of the enquiry.[12]

If one takes this extended Leninist model as the matrix for political philosophy, certain consequences would seem to follow. The first is that it would be a mistake to believe that one could come to any substantive understanding of politics by discussing abstractly the good, the right, the true, or the rational in complete abstraction from the way in which these items figure in the more motivationally active parts of the human psyche, and particularly in abstraction from the way in which they impinge, even if indirectly, on human action. This, in turn, requires an understanding of the existing social and political institutions. In politics "It would be good if . . . (e.g., the tsar were overthrown)" means someone has decided that it would be desirable or advisable if this were to take place, or at any rate has entertained the possibility that this might be done. "Who is that?" is always a pertinent question. It also means that someone is in principle willing to try to implement "the good" that has been determined, even if the form that attempt at implementation takes is a series of weak and ineffectual actions that amount to no more than some seditious conversations, or committing to memory a subversive poem.[13] This in no way implies that there is no such thing as truth. Lenin famously claimed that Marx's theory was powerful *because* it was true, and not the other way around.[14] Still, neither the good nor the true is self-realising, so it is not generally a sufficient explanation of why people believe that X that X is true or of why people do Y that Y is "good."

There is one further element to be found in Lenin's writings that is of special importance for political theory: his discussion of the principle of partisanship.[15] That is his claim that there are only two philosophical ways of looking at the world: materialism and idealism. These are incompatible global theories that constitute the respective correctly understood worldviews of the bourgeoisie and the proletariat, and they are as irreconcilably at war with each other as are their respective hosts. *Every* theory to some extent takes a position in this war; every theory is "partisan." Therefore, intellectual honesty requires that one reflect on the contribution one's theory makes to the class struggle, and acknowledge it openly. One does not have to accept the specific claim that there are two, and only two, mutually exclusive worldviews to one of which any theory must commit itself, to accept the general claim that entertaining, developing, and propounding a theory are actions, and as such they represent ways of taking a position in the world. This means that any kind of comprehensive understanding of politics will also have to treat the politics of theorisation, including the politics of whatever theory is itself at the given time being presented for scrutiny as a candidate for acceptance. One need not assume that "honesty" requires one specifically to elaborate and call attention to the partisan commitments of one's theory in every possible context, because contexts and the legitimate questions to which they give rise differ, and there is nothing in principle wrong with accepting a certain amount of intellectual division of labour.

Still, the general point that a political theory is, among other things, potentially a partisan intervention is well-taken, so questions about the actual political implications of a theory cannot be excluded as in principle irrelevant.

Priorities, Preferences, Timing

That, then, is the first and by far most important of the three questions the conjunction of which in some sense—namely, for the realist view with which I am concerned—maps out the realm of politics. The second question is, by contrast, one that represents not a new line of thought, but something more like an addendum to the first. The best way to think about how the second question arises is to think about Nietzsche's insistence on the finitude of human existence and on the fact that the structure of human valuation is always differential. The model for most politics, according to Nietzsche, should not be that of an irresistible ἔρως that draws individuals on, so that they follow looking neither to the right nor to the left. To the extent to which the pull that moves me really is irresistible, like an invincibly strong addiction, then the normal procedures of evaluation, deliberation, choice, decision, etc., that constitute the substance of our political life are not operating. The same is true of overwhelming aversion. The person being tortured who simply wants it to STOP (PERIOD) is also not a good model for an agent acting politically. Politics as we know it is a matter of differential choice: opting for A *rather than* B.[16] Thus politics is not about doing what is good or rational or beneficial *simpliciter*—it is not even obvious that that is an internally coherent thought at all—but about the pursuit of what is good in a particular concrete case by agents with limited powers and resources, where choice of one thing to pursue means failure to choose and pursue another.

I would like to group here a number of phenomena having to do with order, sequence, priority, and the temporality or historicality of collective action. To propose that we do X is always to propose that we do X rather than any other possible action, or at any rate that we do X before we do something else. In many cases, the specific order in which one makes decisions is of crucial importance for the actual medium-term result. In an ideal discussion (e.g., of the kind envisaged by Habermas) in which one has, as we say, "all the time in the world," it might not make much difference which topic is discussed first because we will eventually make it our task to get to everything, and can revisit topics without restriction in the light of changes in our views. Whether or not that is the case in idealised academic discussion is not a matter I wish to discuss now, but however that might be, in countless cases of political action what comes first is of great importance for obvious reasons. Once I have done something, I have changed the situation, sometimes for good. As the Bush administration in the United States has perhaps learned, once you destroy something like the Iraqi polity, the pieces cannot necessarily be reassembled.

A related aspect of politics is the importance of timing in political action. Successful action, particularly large-scale action of a drastic kind, often depends on making a delicate judgment about what is realistically possible at what point in time, on identifying the καιρός—the moment that must be seized now because it will never recur—seeing when the time is ripe for action and grasping opportunities that will not present themselves again. An ability to pick the crucial moment when action can be successful is an important constituent of one of the skills a good politician exhibits.[17]

All three of the patrons I have named, Lenin, Nietzsche, and Weber, emphasise the importance of this feature. Lenin had no *theory* of this, and in fact it seems obvious that there are very narrow limits to how far one could have a general theory of this kind of specific skill, since by its very nature it is the exercising of highly particularised judgment on what might be a nonrecurrrent situation, but the emphasis one finds in his speeches and writing on performing potentially far-reaching political action only at a specified "right" moment, neither too early nor too late, gives evidence that he was aware of the importance of this skill.

One might imagine that this category would be especially important for political actors who had a specific philosophy of history, like that of Marxism which considers history to be a generally progressive phenomenon. Thus Social Democrats at the beginning of the twentieth century discussed endlessly when the time would be ripe for revolutionary action, i.e., when the economic situation would be sufficiently propitious, the proletariat would be sufficiently "mature," and the party would be psychologically, socially, and politically prepared to act, and eventually to take power. However, it is incorrect to think that this is a specific concern of views that emphasise the progressive nature of history. Marxists, to be sure, worried about whether society was sufficiently developed, but this development was generally considered to be a cumulative and, for all practical purposes, irreversible process, so if you failed this time, that was disappointing, and wasteful, but, on the mainstream view, it was not necessarily tragic, because history was on your side and the conditions for better luck the next time were reliably there. Recognising the importance of choosing the propitious moment might also be characteristic of conceptions completely different from those mentioned above. Skill in timing political action might be thought to be particularly important precisely if I thought of the political world as providing opportunities that would not present themselves again, that is, if I had to discriminate and act on specific features of the situation that could *not* be assumed to be permanent or to recur in an appropriate form. For instance, when a group of U.S. politicians decided that they would try to remove Iraq as an independent agent in world affairs, either by installing there a government that would be reliably subservient to U.S. geopolitical interests, or by destroying the country completely as a political subject capable of making any effective decisions in international affairs at all, it was likely to have been clear to them from the start that they would have to find or create an opportunity for toppling the Ba'thist regime. The attack on the Pentagon and the World Trade Center in 2001 provided a suitable window of opportunity by generating an enormous amount of undiscriminating vengeful energy that could, with sufficient manipulation, be redirected against Iraq, but it was clear that that window would not stay open indefinitely because the desire for revenge in most cases eventually fades away. In a way Lenin's emphasis on timing is a departure from the main line of Marxist theorising, which by the start of the twentieth century had become slightly academic in the pejorative sense of the term. Lenin shifted the focus back from a very general, speculative theory of history to the realities of political practice in particular situations.

Legitimacy

The third question I wish to raise is one with a long history, but in its modern form it is most clearly articulated by Max Weber. Sometimes human beings feel themselves forced to act by overwhelming pressures in their environment, and sometimes we simply give ourselves over to routines and established habits of action. When the pressure to act, however, is relaxed slightly and our routines are interrupted, we are also capable of asking ourselves *why* we should act in one way rather than another, that is, we look for reasons for action and exchange these with one another. Weber speaks of people who are trying to find reasons for action as engaged in looking for "legitimation" of that action. He thought that politics was generally about collective forms of *legitimating* violence, and he had a refreshingly catholic, and normatively undemanding, notion of what "legitimation" was to be taken to be. Thus Weber was even willing to speak of what he called "legitimation via tradition," which was a situation in which one can just barely distinguish there *being* any legitimation of some form of violent behaviour as opposed to its merely being the case that violence of that sort took place "habitually." Weber's idea, of course, was not that politics was in every specific instance about giving or objecting to a particular legitimising argument for a particular act of violence, but, rather, that there was a generalised human order that claimed and had some kind of legitimacy, and part of that legitimacy was, in one or another of a variety of complex and indirect ways, transmitted down to the acts of violence that were perpetrated as a normal part of social interaction. It seems reasonable to widen the focus slightly. Perhaps, as Weber thought, the characteristic of modern states is that they have control over the threat to use certain kinds of concentrated force as their *ultima ratio*, but not all politics is, in its immediate phenomenal reality, about the control of violence. There are, after all, as Weber knew very well, other ways of coordinating human action apart from the use of force. So a more realistic understanding of what is at issue in politics in a wider variety of circumstances would connect it with attempts to provide legitimacy not simply for acts of violence, but for any kinds of collective action, such as deciding voluntarily to build a new road or change to a new unit of measurement (as was done during the French Revolution), or for that matter for any arrangements that could be seen as capable of being changed, controlled, modified, or influenced by human action. This will include institutions, patterns of distribution of access to resources, and other similar things.

The legitimatory mechanisms available in a given society change from one historical period to another, as do the total set of beliefs held by agents, the mechanisms for changing beliefs, or generating new ones (newspapers, universities, etc.), and the forms of widely distributed, socially rooted, moral conceptions. These are all important parts of what makes a given society the society it is. When the pope crowned Charlemagne emperor in AD 800, this legitimising act had very significant political consequences; nothing comparable would have been possible in AD 80, or in 2008. Partly the reason for this is that there is no emperor in 2008, but partly it is that in AD 80 the very idea of the man called "the pope" dispensing political legitimation would not have made much sense to anyone then alive. If one wants to attain a moderately realistic understanding of why a society behaves politically in a certain way, one will have to take account of the specific way the existing forms of legitimation work. There is nothing "realistic" about closing one's eyes to the fact that such warrants for action exist and are taken seriously. This does *not*, of course, mean that they constitute a closed system at any given time, or that everyone shares the same legitimatory beliefs at any given time in any given society—the plebs and the patricians may well continue to differ about that—or that the ability or inability of a political agent to provide a legitimation for a particular policy is the most important fact, or even an important fact, about that policy. The beliefs that lie at the base of forms of legitimation are often as confused, potentially contradictory, incomplete, and pliable as anything else, and they can in principle be manipulated, although in most cases not *ad libitum*. Although they are not mere "reflections" of something else—certainly not *mere* "superstructural reflections of the economic base," as held, for instance, by certain forms of vulgar Marxism— they also do not have a coherence and independence of the wider political and social world that would allow one to treat them completely in abstraction. One cannot, that is to say, sensibly expect to develop a cognitively illuminating *Logik der Weltbilder* (of the kind, for instance, envisaged at one point by Habermas)[18] in which one maps their structure (and development) as purportedly freestanding abstract entities. They are a part of real history, like most of the rest of life.

Tasks of Political Theory

The image of the subject-matter of political philosophy that one finds when one puts together the three elements of the realist view sketched above is rather clear. In the historical period we can survey we find ourselves as finite, vulnerable, mutually dependent creatures who are also independent sources of action and judgment. We are bound to each other by various relations of power, and we try to act in a concerted way under pressure of time and resources, and in such a way as to give some kind of account to ourselves and others about why we are acting in the way we are; within limits, and unless we are preternaturally tolerant or insightful, we expect others to try to give us some kind of similar account of themselves and their actions. The account they give will almost certainly contain some appeal to particular facts about their social environment and historically specific concepts and theories, although they may well not recognise them as such—they may, for instance, think of them as Divine Laws or Obvious Facts or Self-Evident Dictates of Reason or Sheer Common Sense. With this picture in mind one can ask oneself what the task of political philosophy is. This means not only what it might ideally be capable of doing, but also what it in fact has done, how it has in fact informed the social world, and what role it has actually played in politics.

Understanding, Evaluation, Orientation

I would like to discuss this topic under five heads. First of all, one might think that political philosophy was a systematic attempt to understand how the organised forms of acting together in a given society actually work, and to explain why certain decisions are taken, why certain projects fail and others succeed, or why social and political action exhibits the patterns it does. There might, to be sure, be disagreement about what exactly "understanding" was supposed to mean in the case of politics. Is the best we can aspire to a kind of low-level descriptive account of the various ways in which the political systems that we have encountered in the past or the present are actually organised, or can we get beyond this to formulate some generalisations about the types of systems that exist, or can we even find for the realm of politics something like the general laws that hold in the realm of nature, laws that will support counterfactuals and allow us to predict what will occur? Or is this model itself an inappropriate imitation of the study of nature, and is the understanding of politics we should wish to attain more like the understanding of a text or of another human being than like our understanding of the solar system or of the structure of the human body? Can one understand politics without understanding history, especially the history of political thought, and will this distinguish political philosophy from some other kinds of philosophy (such as, perhaps, logic) to which the study of history is not integral? However one might finally decide what the proper form (or forms) of understanding are, this general task does not seem in principle more problematic for political theory than for any of the other human sciences.

It is, however, also a reasonable generalisation about societies we know that the human beings who live in them are not merely cognitive beings, interested only or even primarily in understanding the world around us. Although Aristotle may have been right to claim that a desire to know is part of the fundamental constitution of human nature, if one means by that the constitution of any human society we could easily recognise, Nietzsche is also correct to emphasise that the impulse to evaluate our surroundings, our fellows, and ourselves is at least as deeply rooted in our human nature as is any natural "desire to know." "Der Mensch ist ein abschätzendes Tier."[19] We naturally compare one thing with another in the interests of finding out which one is "tastier," "more pleasing to the eye," "more useful," and so forth. In this respect the study of politics is no different from most other human enterprises. We do not simply want to understand how the apartheid system worked in South Africa in the 1970s; we wish to judge it as being better or worse (in some respect) than other systems. There is no obvious *single* dimension along which we distinguish the good, the bad, the better, the worse, the best. One social system is more productive; another gives better subsidies to its symphony orchestras; a third has an especially perspicuous and flexible legal system. It is an assumption that there is always one single dimension for assessing persons and their actions that has canonical priority. This is the dimension of moral evaluation; "good/evil" is supposed always to trump any other form of evaluation, but that is an assumption, probably the result of the long history of the Christianisation and then gradual de-Christianisation of Europe, which one need not make. Evaluation need not mean moral evaluation, but might include assessments of efficiency (measured in one or another of varying ways), simplicity, perspicuousness, aesthetic appeal, and so on. It is natural for the modern inheritors of the Western tradition of religion and philosophy to think that we know what the "proper" relation is between the desire to know and the desire to evaluate. We do not wish to "judge" or assess our surrounding merely as a kind of expressive activity carelessly projected onto the world, but we wish to evaluate the world "correctly," i.e., in accordance with what it truly is, and the desire to know is directed at determining what the world truly is. Lenin specifically (and correctly) commends this line of thought when he states that revolutionary praxis requires revolutionary theory.[20]

The third point I would like to make is that humans do not merely wish to understand and evaluate the world around them; it is often claimed that humans' need for general orientation in action is at least as important as the wish for piecemeal understanding or assessment. This has generally been taken to mean one of several slightly different things. Nineteenth-century discussions often emphasise that people wish to lead a "meaningful" life, and then connect this with some kind of desire for a sense of locatedness or having a place in the world. There is then often a shift from this to the further idea that people need a representation or a surveyable image of their place in the world. Sometimes this desire for orientation is construed as what is called a "metaphysical need," and an attempt is made to argue that they need a world-picture or worldview, a theory or image of the world *as a whole*.[21] A further sense in which I can speak of looking for an orientation is not connected with having a general picture or a sense of the meaningfulness of the world, but with having a clear and motivationally effective set of principles and directives about how to act in life, what do to, or perhaps about what goals I should pursue. People who do not know how they should act in a situation are more likely to experience frustration, confusion, or fear; Durkheim called this state *anomie*.[22] To say that I have a sense of the locatedness of my life or that I have relatively clear principles and goals—I know what I think I "ought" to do—does not in itself necessarily imply that I can see my own life in a positive light. Slaves in the ancient world, one can assume, often had a clear sense of their "place"—we might think, too clear a sense of their place—and they rarely suffered from *anomie*, but this did not mean that they were able to see the life they were living as having positive value, or, to use a nineteenth-century expression, to "affirm themselves" in it. This final stage of the argument was, then, often a prelude to some kind of rehabilitation of monotheistic religion or of some philosophical *Weltanschauung* that was an analogue of such a religion. Monotheistic religions in the West have tended to conflate having a general orientation in life, having a specific theory of the world, having a sense of the positive meaningfulness of one's existence, and having a fixed set of rules for behaviour, but these elements are in principle separable. As both Marx and Nietzsche pointed out, it is completely unclear why I can't have a sense of my place in the world simply by being embedded and participating in its practices, *provided* these practices were sufficiently satisfactory, without having a single general representation of why it all makes sense. Marx in particular seemed to hold that having a sense of positive meaningfulness in one's life was a question of acting and interacting, especially of participating in social, productive activities, rather than of having a theory of any kind. The "metaphysical need," in any case, both Marx and Nietzsche held, is a historical phenomenon that arises under determinate circumstances, and could be expected to disappear under other circumstances that we could relatively easily envisage.

Humans in modern societies are driven by a perhaps desperate hope that they might find some way of mobilising their theoretical and empirical knowledge and their evaluative systems so as both to locate themselves and their projects in some larger imaginative structure that makes sense to them, and to guide their actions to bring about what they would find to be satisfactory (or at any rate "less unsatisfactory") outcomes or to improve in some other way the life they live. Furthermore, many modern agents would like it to be the case that the form of orientation which their life has is, if not "true," at least compatible with the best available knowledge, and they would like the principles by which they guide their action to be in some kind of contact with reality, although anyone would be hard put to say precisely what was meant by that. Both the extent to which this hope is present in a certain group and the extent to which it can be realised are empirical matters, although one would have to be extremely sanguine to expect it to be realised to any significant extent.

Conceptual Innovation

The fourth task that political philosophy might perform is one of making a constructive contribution to politics by conceptual invention or innovation. Political agents can face a variety of different kinds of problematic situation. Let me start with two cases. Sometimes people think they know rather clearly what immediate goals they wish to attain, and also know what powers, means, or resources would have to be at their disposal if they were to have a chance of attaining the goals. Thus a political party might know they would like to enact a certain piece of legislation and also know they need a certain number of votes from members of one of the opposition parties to carry the legislation; the problem is how to get them. One might think that what the party needs here is what some have called "technical" or "instrumental" knowledge. Of course, from the fact that one might say they "need" this knowledge, it does not follow that any such knowledge in fact exists, any more than it follows from the fact that I say a man in the desert needs water that any water is at all potentially available to him. A second possible case is one in which the members of some group do not know which of a number of pregiven proposals is best, either best for their immediate or long-term interests, or "best" in some other sense. Here one might naturally be inclined to say that they need help in assessing the given options.

In addition to these two kinds of case, however, there are also indeterminately many other kinds of problematic situation, and many of them are difficult to discuss because the problem itself is often not clearly visible as a problem until one has the answer or a possible set of answers. People, that is, can be at a loss what to do or fail to know what they want because they are confused about what is wrong or what the problem precisely is. They do not understand the situation in which they find themselves, and so don't even know what they should be looking for. In such cases, it is sometimes possible that a certain kind of conceptual innovation may help them. Political theory might (in some cases) discharge the function of providing a new thought-instrument or conceptual tool to help particular people understand and define, and thus begin to deal with, certain problems. The archetypical case I have in mind here is the early modern invention of the concept of "the state" as an abstract structure of power and authority distinct both from the population and from the prince, aristocracy, or ruling class, which successfully enforces a monopoly of legitimate violence within a certain territory.[23] Proposing to think about politics through employing the concept of "the state" in a central place in one's theory is not like offering a solution to the difficulties that confronted the agents in the two initial examples discussed above.

"Conceptual innovation" in the sense intended is not much like simply introducing a new lexical item into speech to designate something that already exists, as when people decided to call a certain illness that was afflicting the population "bubonic plague," or, for that matter, it is not like giving a simple name to something that does not (yet) exist, as when Mr. Biro, the inventor of the ballpoint pen, might have sat down to try to invent a writing instrument that he proposed to name after himself. In interesting cases, like "the state," introducing the "concept" requires one to get people not merely to use a certain word, but also to entertain a certain kind of theory, which has a strong "normative" component. You don't "have" the concept of the state unless you have the idea of a freestanding form of *authority*. and the idea of authority requires some appeal to notions like "ought" or "should." You do not automatically have a state when some group of people *in fact* completely controls the use of violence within a territory—if you did, every group of successful kidnappers would constitute a "state." Rather, a state exists only if enough people think they "ought" to obey the orders of some person or designated group of people, in the right sense of "ought." The sense of "ought" in question might be indeterminate in certain ways, but it must certainly go beyond the sense of "ought" implicit in saying, "You ought to do what he says," meaning that since he is holding a gun to your head, it would be exceedingly inadvisable to fail to do what he requests. Characteristically, the concept "the state" is introduced *together with* a theory about the nature and the source of the authority which the abstract entity that is so named is supposed to have. In the early modern period this was usually some version of the social contract theory. Of course, once the state actually gets established as a distinct and massive social reality that cannot be ignored, one can come to reflect that the purported sources of its "authority" are deficient, that the social contract theory is invalid, false, or confused, and one might even come to the conclusion that the state "ought" to have no real authority. To say this retrospectively, that is, to call an entity that was in some sense originally introduced by being *defined* as a locus of authority "nonauthoritative," is, under the circumstances, no more problematic than continuing to call Greenland "Greenland" even after one discovers that it is not, after all—or, at any rate, was not until the recent acceleration of global warming—very green.

When they were introduced, concepts like "the state" did not exactly mirror any fully preexisting reality, because using these concepts represented as much an aspiration as a description. It is also the case that merely *using* the concepts did not *by itself*, without the assistance of real social forces that actually act in history, bring any state into existence; neither concepts nor theories realise themselves. Nevertheless inventing this new concept, in this case by transforming the meaning of existing terms such as *status/estat/stato*, could be an important contribution both to clarifying an obscure situation and to guiding action directed at institutional change. Having the "concept" (in the requisite sense, including the various theory-fragments that were associated with it) meant that one saw certain problems clearly, namely, the problems of ensuring political order in an incipiently atomised society without recourse to religion, and it also meant that one had a solution, or at any rate a suggestion for a solution that one could try to put to work. Having the concept of "the state" could give one, then, an important analytic tool that could allow one to think more clearly about social processes in train, and could help one to see what actions are required.

Sometimes conceptual innovations work, take hold, and flourish in the world, the mind, and the imagination. Vivid examples of this include "the state" and "democracy" (a term originally coined sometime in the mists of the sixth century BC, which was politically active for a couple of centuries, and was then put away on the shelf for two thousand years to be resurrected and redefined out of all recognition in the early twentieth century).[24] When such innovations work, they imprint themselves on the world. "The state" is now not merely a concept but a social reality. If Nietzsche's account in *Zur Genealogie der Moral* is at all correct, the concept of "evil" is a similar kind of conceptual innovation that has put down roots and created a psychic, and somatic, reality to which it now refers. Sometimes, to be sure, innovative conceptual constructs do not work (as in the case of *phalanstère*, *Führerprinzip*, "the Third Way," or "the dictatorship of the proletariat"). Conceptual innovation in the sense in question here is a complicated process in which descriptive, analytic, normative, and aspirational elements are intricately intertwined. What it means in each case to say that a particular conceptual proposal did not work is, thus, a complicated question to which, probably, only a detailed historically specific answer can be given. Sometimes the failure seems to result directly from the cognitive deficiencies of the proposed innovation: the Third Way had no content and was useless as an analytic or cognitive tool, so it was swiftly seen to be a mere exercise in attaching a brand-label to various disparate policies developed by the first New Labour government, and the use of the term was abandoned. Sometimes the proposal wasn't sufficiently attractive or plausible to enough people for it to be given a real chance, such as in the case of the *phalanstères*. Sometimes the cause of failure is not clear. Did the *Führerprinzip* fail because it was analytically or cognitively deficient, because too many humans could not tolerate the consequences of accepting it, or because of the military defeat of the Third Reich? Or because of some combination of all three?

To repeat, having the *idea* of the state does not automatically ensure that one has a proper, full understanding of what having a state would or does imply, nor, as has already been mentioned, does it ensure that a state really exists. The reason is clear: for there to be a state there must exist an actual concentration of power of a certain kind that does not always exist, and probably could not exist in certain historical periods. Equally, however, because a state is a conjunction of concentrated power and a certain kind of abstract authority, there is a sense in which one could not "really" have *the state*, unless one had a minimally proper and not completely deviant concept of it. "State authority" is not the kind of thing that can exist independently of some form of conceptualisation.

The references above to conceptual tools might suggest that one should think of this as a kind of "pragmatic" task for political philosophy, but there are some important differences between the paradigmatic cases I have in mind here and everyday cases of "pragmatic" problem solving. First, in everyday cases one usually knows what the problem is before looking for the solution, as in the two cases described at the very start of this section. In many of the cases of conceptual innovation that I have in mind, creating the conceptual tools is a precondition to coming to a clear understanding of what the problem was in the first place. It is very difficult to describe the transition after it has taken place because it is difficult for us to put ourselves back into the situation of confusion, indeterminacy, and perplexity that existed before the new "tool" brought clarity, and this means it is difficult for us to retain a vivid sense of what a difference having the concept made. We can just barely imagine ourselves in a world in which there are no states, as opposed to local barons, warlords, clans, primitive communal forms of village organisation, etc. Some forms of Kantianism put great weight on "what we can imagine," holding that this can be a source of insight into necessary connections. Thus various of Kant's arguments about space and time depend on the purported fact that it is impossible for us to imagine certain things: we can know, Kant claims, a priori that space has only three dimensions because we cannot imagine it as having more than three dimensions. History in the form of non-Euclidean geometry and modern physics has put paid to that particular line of argument, but in general we should beware of depending too much on "what we can imagine," especially in politics. As Nietzsche puts it somewhere, sometimes the fact that you can't imagine a situation in which things are very different from the way they are now is not an especially good argument for the claim that they *must* be as they now are, but, rather, represents a failure of your powers about which you should feel mildly apologetic. Sometimes the right response to "But I can't *imagine* that" is "Oh yes, you can. Please just try harder"; sometimes the right response is "Yes, I see that you can't, poor thing, perhaps we can get you some help."

There is a second difference between conceptual innovation and the pragmatic invention of tools. When we use a tool in everyday life, it usually remains a detached instrument under my control and activated only when, where, and how I decide. I tie some catnip to the end of a broom handle to lure Tabitha down off the roof, but when that episode is finished, I either decompose the new tool (the "cat-lure") completely or put it away under the stairs: Tabitha is off the roof; nothing else has changed. Given the extremely rudimentary nature of her general mental processes and the weakness of her memory, it is not even guaranteed that she won't find herself back up in the same place on the roof again tomorrow, mewing piteously in the same way as today. In contrast, conceptual innovations often "stick," escape our control and become part of reality itself. Once Hobbes invents the idea of the "state," this idea can come into contact with real social forces with unforeseeable results. The "tool" develops a life of its own, and can become an inextricable part of the fabric of life itself.[25] "The state" might be a conceptual innovation invented to deal with a certain real problem (that of demonstrating how to ensure self-preservation and an order of a certain kind), but regardless of Hobbes's own views, it quickly attracts to itself independent loyalty, so that in the end people are willing to sacrifice their lives for it. Often you can't see the original problem clearly until you have the conceptual instrument, but having the instrument can then change the "real" situation with which one is confronted so that other, unforeseen problems emerge.

Ideology

The fifth possible function of political theory is more controversial. Many theorists have held that political theories have had the further function of either propounding and fostering, or that they ought to have the function of analysing and helping to dissolve, ideologies.[26] If the earlier discussion is correct, power in its various forms is an important feature of human societies. When we think of power, we most naturally and immediately think of relatively direct ways in which it is employed. An adult has the power to pick up a package that weighs one kilo; a national government exercises its power by locking up those who break the law; a large firm that is struggling with a number of competitors to increase its market share uses its financial power to buy out and eliminate one or two of these competitors. One characteristic of the use of power here, a characteristic that makes it rather easy to identify the exercise of power, is that it is being used to overcome some kind of distinct visible resistance: the weight of the package, the attempts on the part of lawbreakers to evade or escape the attentions of the police, the various actions of the competing firms before they are eliminated. Power, however, can also be used indirectly to shape opinions, attitudes, and desires, and thus to manufacture what looks like "consent," and in this form, many have wanted to claim, it is not so easily visible. Thus the arms industry can use its financial power to influence newspapers in the direction of generating a climate of fear that will be conducive to higher governmental expenditures on weapons, or oil companies can fund research directed at demonstrating that global warming is not caused by the burning of fossil fuels. In a society in which powerful social agencies have a strong interest in commercializing as many aspects of human life as possible and have succeeded to a considerable extent in implementing this interest, it would not be surprising if people came to think that the existence of a "free market" in health care, education, organ transplanting, or the adoption of children was "natural" and required no further comment, scrutiny, or explanation. This belief would be a reflection of how things appeared to be (in their society). Such effects of power can be less visible because they operate on amorphous initial states rather than against distinctly constituted opposition; after all, who "initially" would have any view whatever about the connection between global warming and fossil fuels? People will also be unlikely to have very well-formed beliefs about how organ transplants are organized until the society comes to have a technological way of performing such transplants. How exactly power relations operate to generate or influence the formation of beliefs, desires, and attitudes is a complex question, and there will probably be little of much significance one will be able to say in general about the mechanisms by which this influence is exercised. Only a historical account of the particular details of the case will be at all enlightening. In some central and important cases, however, so the proponents of the theory of "ideology" argue, the existence of specific power relations in the society will produce an appearance of a particular kind. Certain features of the society that are merely local and contingent, and maintained in existence only by the continual exercise of power, will come to seem as if they were universal, necessary, invariant, or natural features of all forms of human social life, or as if they arose spontaneously and uncoercedly by free human action. A "free market" requires constant intervention by powerful social agencies if it is to maintain itself in existence, but in a society in which that constant intervention has been overwhelmingly successful and its forms traditional, people's basic beliefs and desires will have become channeled[27] so that the "market" comes to seem natural. If this happens, then agents who have a particular interest in the maintenance of the market (e.g., companies that profit by providing private health services) will be in a position to present what are in fact merely their particular interests as universal interests.

An ideology, then, is a set of beliefs, attitudes, preferences that are distorted as a result of the operation of specific relations of power; the distortion will characteristically take the form of presenting these beliefs, desires, etc., as inherently connected with some universal interest, when in fact they are subservient to particular interests. One can think of an ideology as a composite comprising three elements:

1. a certain configuration of power;

2. this configuration of power brings it about that certain contingent, variable features of our human mode of ex-

istence (which are in fact maintained in existence only by the constant exercise of that power) appear to be universal, "natural," or necessary or spontaneously arising features;

3. as a result of (2), certain particular interests can plausibly present themselves as universal ones.

If ideologies exist, that is, if the term has any real use at all, then it would seem that a political theory or political philosophy could be related to a given ideology in at least two distinct ways. One possibility would be that a political philosophy could play a progressive role in combating ideological illusion, such as when the philosophy in question demonstrates the dependence of certain beliefs or desires on the continued existence of particular configurations of power that would otherwise remain hidden. This is philosophy as "criticism of ideology." A second possibility is that a political theory or philosophy itself played an ideological role in society in that it fostered certain common ideological illusions, made them more difficult to detect, or created new ones, e.g., the idea that New Labour could represent a Third Way, or that all people in every society everywhere aspire before all else to a particular kind of "democratic" political culture. The ideological role can be relatively active or relatively passive; that is, a political theory can actively promote a certain conceptual confusion or an ideological appearance, or, negatively, it can divert attention away from the dependency of some form of consciousness on a particular configuration of power. A political theory can in principle divert attention from the distorting influence of relations of power without its even being the case that some part of the content of the theory, narrowly construed, is false, wrong, or incorrect. Diverting attention from the way in which certain beliefs, desires, attitudes, or values are the result of particular power relations, then, can be a sophisticated way of contributing to the maintenance of an ideology, and one that will be relatively immune to normal forms of empirical refutation. If I claim (falsely) that all human societies, or all human societies at a certain level of economic development, have a free market in health services, that is a claim that can be demonstrated to be false. On the other hand, if I focus your attention in a very intense way on the various different tariffs and pricing schema that doctors or hospitals or drug companies impose for their products and services, and if I become morally outraged by "excessive" costs some drug companies charge, discussing at great length the relative rates of profit in different sectors of the economy, and pressing the moral claims of patients, it is not at all obvious that anything I say may be straightforwardly "false"; after all, who knows what "excessive" means? However, by proceeding in this way I might well focus your attention on narrow issues of "just" pricing, turning it away from more pressing issues about the acceptance in some societies of the very existence of a free market for drugs and medical services. One can even argue that the *more* outraged I become about the excessive price, the more I obscure the underlying issue. One way, then, in which a political philosophy can be ideological is by presenting a relatively marginal issue as if it were central and essential. The (mis)direction of limited human attention in this case would be the analogue in the theoretical sphere of the Nietzschean issues of "priority" discussed above.

If ideologies exist, it does not seem outrageous to assume that analyzing and criticizing them is a reputable task for a political theory. This scheme of five possible tasks that emerges, then, is rather crude, and to be completely convincing it would have to be elaborated and qualified in various ways. In particular understanding, evaluation, and guidance are complexly connected in ways one would have to discuss. However, as a first approximation we will assume that all five of these goals or functions for political philosophy are unobjectionable.

Part II
Failures of Realism

One might worry that the form of "realism" described in the foregoing is so broadly construed as to be vacuous, excluding nothing. As with Reason, Mother's Love, the Internet, or The Idea of the Good, it is hard to be against "being realistic." The preliminary sketch given in Part I of this book might usefully be further clarified through a contrast between it and two influential contemporary views that represent almost the direct opposite of "realism" in the sense in which I wish to understand the term. One fashionable way of failing to be realistic is to try to construct a society along the lines of an idealised legal system structured around a set of rights. Another way is to develop a full political theory by picking a single purported political "virtue" from among the many human excellences and aspects of politics or society that are admirable; one tries to give an abstract "conceptual analysis" of "our" conception of that virtue without taking account of the social context in which it is instantiated or its history, and then constructs an idealised theory of what a society would have to look like if it were to instantiate that virtue fully. A "realist" in the sense in which I am using the term will, contrary to this, start from an account of our existing motivations and our political and social institutions (not from a set of abstract "rights" or from our intuitions). The full and illuminating description of these institutions and practices will require use of an evaluative vocabulary with a certain history. Then one can go on from there. The two examples of nonrealistic approaches are merely examples and are not intended to exhaust the possible ways in which a theory can fail to be appropriately realistic. Each of the two examples fails, among other reasons, because each tries to ignore or blank out history, sociology, and the particularities that constitute the substance of any recognisable form of human life. Each has an unreflective and uncritical relation to "our" concepts or "our (moral) intuitions," and this turns out to result in serious cognitive deficiencies.

Rights

To start with the first of my two examples, the notion of an "individual right" plays such an important role in our society that it has come to seem perfectly natural to us to assume that the basic framework for thinking about politics is a set of properly constituted rights, either legal rights or some more vaguely envisaged "human" rights. If this is the best way to proceed, and rights really are so central to understanding politics, it might be thought important to get clear about what a "right" is.

Historians make a broad distinction between what they call "objective" and "subjective" conceptions of "rights."[28] Roughly speaking, an "objective" conception is one that takes the basic content of the "right" in question to be one that is best expressed by statements of the form "It is right that children obey their parents," or "It is not right to leave the dead unburied," or "It is right to worship the gods in the customarily prescribed way," or "It is not right to lie in court or Parliament," or, finally, "It is right that debtors pay their debts." These are general statements that describe a form of social interaction which is presented as an object of approval and is positively enjoined either on anyone indeterminately (in the second and third cases) or on anyone who fulfils the necessary conditions (such as, in the first case, being a child, in the fourth being a witness, juror, or Member of Parliament, in the fifth being a debtor). From this formulation it is not at all clear whose "responsibility," as one might say, it is to bury any particular dead person or to organise the proper worship of the gods, but this in no way throws into question the validity of the claim about what is right. The case is further complicated because in contemporary English we use the phrase "It is right" in a very wide range of cases, including what is socially appropriate and decorous ("It is right to greet your hostess before speaking to the other guests"), what is advisable on various pragmatic grounds ("It is right to get that property surveyed before you make a bid for it"), what is morally demanded ("It is right to return lost property, even if the owner cannot document a claim to it"), and what is legally required ("It is right to wear seatbelts while driving or riding in a car"). So to speak of a "right" (in the objective sense) is to speak of a legal-juridical requirement or a shadowy moral-religious analogue of such a legal requirement, or even a point of etiquette, protocol, or a general piece of good advice considered as if it were some kind of metaphorical requirement imposed on minimally rational and well-socialised people. To say the conception is "objective" is to say that it is *not* thought of primarily relative to some particular bearer of the right. "It is right to spare the temples of the gods during times of war" is a general prescription about how society ought to work, but does not clearly specify any one particular person or group of people to whom a bundle of claims/ powers/obligations/freedoms (etc.) is to be assigned.

This is a very different way of construing "rights" from the so-called subjective conception, which starts from the idea that there is a set of powers and obligations that is essentially construed as located in a particular "subject." The paradigmatic model for the subjective conception is not "It is wrong to lie to Parliament" or "It is right that laws intended to apply to everyone be publicly promulgated," but "I have a right to (life, freedom, this piece of property, etc.)." Those who distinguish between objective and subjective conceptions hold that to say, "It is right that theft be severely punished," is very different conceptually from saying that Jane has a right to leave the city if she so wishes. Objective conceptions of "right" construe "right" as a kind of adverb, modifying *ways* in which social interactions can take place; subjective conceptions construe "right" as a kind of noun— one can even speak of "a right" or "two rights," as if rights could be individuated and counted, as in the phrase "when two rights collide"—with a deeply rooted connection to a human who purportedly "has" the right. The subjective conception is already halfway down the path to thinking about individuals as "holders," possessors, or "owners" of rights. Many modern legal systems are set up so as to ascribe to individuals particular rights, and it is not problematic to say what that means if the legal systems in question are really in operation. "I have a right to live in this house" means that the British courts will instruct the police to prevent my neighbours from ejecting me from my house should they try to do this. These are sometimes called "positive" rights because they are specified and positively enforced by an actually existing legal system.

In many modern philosophical theories a person is thought to have some minimal subjective rights that are not "positive" rights, in that they are not effectively enforced by any existing legal apparatus. In fact these rights are thought of as being "prior" to their codification and enforcement by any given operational legal system. People are thought to have these rights merely by virtue of some property that is inherent in being a human subject at all. What that property is, has shown itself to be remarkably difficult to specify, but since I think that the whole conception of a "subjective right" that is not a right ascribed positively to an individual by a functioning legal system is confused, this does not surprise me. Some of the candidates for the property of a human subject by virtue of which that subject comes to be a bearer of rights include being a child of God, being (potentially) autonomous, being a chooser, being rational, being capable of having a life-plan. A consequence of this is thought to be that *all* humans are the bearers of such rights, and it is not hard to see why this addition seems naturally attractive. If a subjective right is something one has *simply* by virtue of some feature or property that is inherent in being a subject at all, then all humans will have that feature. Depending on the feature or property in question, one might still have some difficulties. Certain kinds of mentally ill persons might not meet the requirements of rationality, but, so the argument runs, these can be treated as exceptional cases that do not affect the central claim about the universal distribution of subjective rights. This notion of a set of "subjective" individual rights that are lodged in *all* humans is very familiar to modern inhabitants of Western Europe, and it is mightily reinforced in its hold on all of us by all the institutions of a commercial society, and by legal codes deriving from the great political transformations of the late eighteenth century that encoded the "right to (this-and-that)" in the very legal structure of society.

The twentieth-century philosopher Robert Nozick explicitly rests the whole of his political philosophy on this familiar conception of an individual subjective right. In the much-quoted first sentence of his book *Anarchy, State, and Utopia*[29] he writes, "Individuals have rights, and there are things no person or group may do to them (without violating their rights)" (p. ix). He then allows that bald statement to lie flapping and gasping for breath like a large, moribund fish on the deck of a trawler, with no further analysis or discussion, and proceeds to draw consequences from it. Presumably the statement actually means "*All* human individuals have rights, etc.," although that is never specifically stated. The existence of rights that (all) individuals "have" is, he seems to think, to be taken for granted, and requires no further argumentative support. The theory of such rights is the lens through which one must learn to "see the political realm" (p. x) as a whole, and is the foundation both of (normative) political philosophy and of explanatory political theory.

Many criticisms have been directed at the details of Nozick's position, both at the particular set of individual rights he assigns to humans and at the consequences he draws from his assumptions.[30] I would like to take a slightly different tack and ask why one should *assume* that the proper starting point for political philosophy should be a set of subjective rights at all. Why should we make that assumption? One possibility might be that we simply could not imagine any way of going about social life other than one based on some distribution of "(subjective) rights," but that seems simply false. We can imagine such a state because we know that it did actually exist. It seems an incontrovertible historical fact that the very concept of a "subjective right" in anything like its modern form is an invention of the late Middle Ages.[31] In particular, historians have argued that this conception arose during the discussion about the so-called *vita apostolica*. Certain members of the religious order of "Franciscans" claimed that the perfect life was a life that imitated as closely as possible the life of Jesus. Since Jesus, they claimed, lived a life of complete poverty, all members of their order should equally aspire to such a life. The "apostolic life" therefore was a life in which one "owned" literally nothing. During the course of an exceedingly complex, indirect, obscure, but fascinating discussion extending over decades, if not centuries, the notion of a "subjective right" gradually emerged from reflections on the very coherence of living such an "apostolic life." Appeal to the idea of a subjective right allowed one to say that a Franciscan might in fact make "use" of various things—might consume food, wear a tunic, or carry a water-bottle—without making any claim to a subjective right, either of ownership or of use, over those necessary things.

There is disagreement about the extent to which the Romans might have had individual legal categories that contained the germs which were eventually to develop into a doctrine of "subjective rights," but it is clear that the ancient Greeks had no concept at all that corresponded to this conception. It is not even linguistically possible to formulate the statement "I have a right to . . . (for example) life" in fifth-century Greek in any natural and transparent way. One can, of course, say, "It is not right/just/proper/lawful that you kill me now," but, of course, that is precisely the point: this formulation translates the expression of a subjective right into an objective idiom.

It seems extremely implausible to respond to this by saying, "Well, they may not have had the *concept* of a subjective right, but that does not mean that the reality did not exist." Europeans may not have had a "concept" of the colour "turquoise" or the concept of a marsupial before a certain time, but it does not follow from that that the colour turquoise did not exist or never was instantiated before that time or that there were no marsupials (albeit in the Antipodes where no European penetrated until the seventeenth century). This seems perfectly plausible in the case of kangaroos and exotic flora, but can one really be said to have a concept of something like "rights" if one does not have the reality of a legal system that is to some extent kept distinct from social or religious custom and moral sentiment, and also if there is no indication that the agents in question are aware of and mark this difference? As with the "state" having the reality does seem in some minimal sense to require having some way of conceptualising it.

Modern philosophers might also be tempted by the thought that if one can in general translate "I have a right to life" into "It is never right/just/proper that anyone kill me," then what difference does it make whether one has an objective or a subjective conception? Doesn't it really amount to a merely different way of putting the same thing? I think not. Even if it were true—which it is not—that every individual statement expressed in the language of subjective rights could be adequately translated into a statement in the language of objective rights (and vice versa), this would still not mean that the particular way in which rights were conceived—objectively or subjectively—was philosophically irrelevant. Part of the reason for this is that the "objective" formulation of Nozick's basic thesis would draw attention to aspects of his view that might otherwise escape scrutiny. If instead of "Individuals have rights and there are things no one can do to them (without violating those rights)," the basic thesis read, "It is right that a certain bundle of powers/freedoms/immunities be assigned to each individual," this immediately raises the question of *why* this is (objectively) right, i.e., why this is the "right" way to organise social interaction, what the exact nature of the bundle of powers and immunities is, what it means to say they are "assigned" to each individual, who it is who does the assigning. "Individuals have rights and there are things no one can do to them (without violating those rights)" is a philosophical dead end; asking what particular immunities it would make sense to assign (in some specific sense of "assign") to which individuals in this historical context is, in contrast, both philosophically and politically a more fruitful question.

Showing that some past human societies lacked a concept of subjective rights altogether, and tracing the way in which that concept developed contingently through history does not in any way "refute" the concept; that is, it does not demonstrate that it is in any way incoherent or defective, and it certainly does not show that we should, or even could, get rid of it. It would, of course, refute certain beliefs, tacit or explicit, which we might have about the concept, for instance the belief that the concept was *so* natural and indispensable that one could not imagine that a society might lack it. Demonstrating that subjective rights were a local invention of postmedieval Europe would also in no way invalidate the claim that it would be a good idea for every society to institute and impose a regime of individual legal rights, and encourage the members of the society to use the concept of a subjective right as widely as possible. Philosophers call the claim that reference to the genesis, history, or development of a view has some refutational force "the genetic fallacy," and in the form in which these alleged "genetic refutations" are usually presented in the philosophical literature they are correctly described as "fallacies." However, the immediate disqualification of historical arguments as instances of "the genetic fallacy" often misses the point that a historical narrative is intended to make. Historical arguments often have a completely different aim and structure from purported refutations. They are not in the first instance intended to support or refute a thesis; rather, they aim to change the structure of argument by directing attention to a new set of relevant questions that need to be asked. They are contributions not to finding out whether this or that argument is invalid or poorly supported, but to trying to *change* the questions people ask about concepts and arguments. One of the effects that one type of historical account ought to have is that of causing it to seem naïve or "unphilosophical" simply to make a certain set of assumptions. If very many different kinds of societies, some of them of significant complexity, lack the very idea of a subjective right, why *assume* with no further argument that subjective rights are a natural part of the framework for political thinking? No amount of cleverness in looking for solutions to puzzles, such as how it is that original acquisition gives someone the "right" to a piece of property, will be enlightening if one is asking the wrong question. Historical enquiry will not by itself necessarily ensure that one asks the right ones, but it can contribute to helping to avoid certain ways of thinking that will lead only to confusion. The reasons why we have most of the political and moral concepts we have (in the forms in which we have them) are contingent, historical reasons, and only a historical account will give us the beginnings of understanding of them and allow us to reflect critically on them rather than simply taking them for granted.

So political philosophy should become more historical, or, rather, it should recognise explicitly that it has always had an important historical dimension that, to its cost, it has tried its best to ignore. "All individuals obviously have rights; let's see what follows from that" is not a good starting point for philosophical reflection. However, some historically more specific questions are good starting points. These include the following: "Is it possible to organise a 'complex modern' society without the use of the concept of a 'right,' and if it is impossible, why is it impossible?" or "What is it about *our* specific form of society that makes 'individual rights' so convenient and plausible? What are the advantages (and disadvantages) of this?" or "If we find it hard to imagine a society without subjective rights, or hard to imagine that *we* could live a full and rich life in such a society, why is that the case? What exactly puts us off?" This is not reducing philosophy to history, but replacing a rather useless set of questions with a potentially more interesting and fruitful set. It is not that Nozick got something wrong by specifying the wrong set of rights or making mistakes of argumentation, but that he does not ask the right questions, and by presenting "rights" as the self-evident basis for thinking about politics, he actively distracts people from asking other, highly relevant questions. It is not that there is some *other* foundation for all thinking or even all "normative" thinking about human society, namely, some foundation that does not appeal to "subjective rights." Rather, why assume that one can begin to think at all systematically and to any effect without being critical about the assumption that politics needs foundations of this kind? Being appropriately critical about this requires that one be historically informed.

Justice

The second example of a nonrealist political philosophy is John Rawls's early theory as presented in his *A Theory of Justice* (1971). Again I am not in the first instance interested in the details of Rawls's view here but wish to treat him merely as a representative of a particular style of theorising about politics.[32]

Rawls begins his political philosophy not with a substantive account of human nature and its exigencies, of the demands that collective action imposes on us, or of purportedly basic or historically constituted human social and political institutions, but with the analysis of the concept of "justice" as a freestanding social ideal. He proposes a theory in three parts. First, he claims that justice has a kind of absolute standing. *A Theory of Justice* begins with this assertion: "Justice is the first virtue of social institutions, as truth is of systems of thought. A theory however elegant and economical must be rejected or revised if it is untrue; likewise laws and institutions no matter how efficient and well-arranged must be reformed or abolished if they are unjust. . . . [T]ruth and justice are uncompromising" (p. 3). How, one might ask, do we know that justice has this preeminence? Rawls's second basic claim is that we have a particular kind of access to this preeminence: we have an "intuitive conviction of the primacy of justice" (*TJ*, p. 4) over all other considerations including welfare, efficiency, democratic choice, transparency, dignity, international competitiveness, or freedom, and, of course, over any rooted moral, philosophical, or religious conceptions. There is no account of where these intuitions came from, whether they might be in any way historically or sociologically variable, or what role they play in society.

The third part of Rawls's position is his theory of the "original position" and the choice of principles of justice "under the veil of ignorance." To understand what the content of justice is, one must imagine people hypothetically joining together to choose once and for all the basic terms on which they will live together, that is, the basic institutions and practices that will constitute their society. These agents "choose," but, in order to exclude the possibility of the unwarranted influence of some over others, they may not discuss their choice with anyone else. The people in question are said to choose "under the veil of ignorance" because Rawls further imagines them to be making their choice in ignorance of the state of economic development of the society in which they will live, its concrete history, their concrete identities, and their position in the society that will result from their decision. It is a fundamental assumption of the view, although no special attention is directed to pointing out that it is an assumption, that the disembodied "agents" who are described in this thought experiment can be construed as making anything we could even recognise as a "choice" at all. "Choice under the veil of ignorance," many have argued, is an incoherent concept. How can "I," or anyone else, be said to choose, if I have been specifically deprived of knowledge of most of what gives me grounds or reasons for making any choice: my empirical identity, my age, economic position, whatever general philosophical orientation or worldview I might have, knowledge of my place in history and my affective relations? Furthermore, why is it assumed that the agents in the original position will agree in choosing anything at all, especially if discussion is prohibited? Why assume that "choice" under the specified circumstances will exhibit any kind of convergence at all? It is further assumed that the agents can be said to be choosing "principles"—rather than, for instance, simply designating someone as Head Man, Big Chief, *Pater Patriae*, Grand Dragon, or what have you, and doing whatever this person says. Finally, Rawls believes that this choice of "principles" can be appropriately described as a choice of the content that the concept of "justice" will have for those who choose. Under these circumstances, Rawls thinks—and with this one returns to the explicit part of his theory—that the "people" in question will agree that justice consists in fairness and that fairness consists in conformity to a complex system of principles, which are designed to ensure an equal distribution of liberties, opportunities, basic rights, and duties to all members of the society in question. Finally, the system contains an escape clause that permits departure from economic equality under certain conditions if this is "necessary" in order to increase the level of welfare of those least well off.

The "original position" is obviously not at all a very good model for political deliberation or action, among other reasons because there is no discussion and no καιρός in it. This is not, as it were, a feature Rawls has overlooked, but it is part of his intention because the "original position" was supposed to be disjoined from real politics, an ideal standpoint from which to survey the human world disinterestedly and impartially.

There are a number of questions that this approach immediately raises. Is it, for instance, true that "we" have an "intuitive conviction of the primacy of justice"? Do we even have a clear, agreed-on concept of "justice" that is the shared kernel of whatever intuitive beliefs we might have about it and its place in politics? Even if it were true that we had an intuition of the primacy a certain particular concept of justice has, is it obviously best to begin a discussion of political philosophy by taking *that intuition* as the starting point and trying to make the whole domain of politics cohere with that intuition? Is Rawls's proposed mechanism of "choice in the original position under a veil of ignorance" for determining the content of justice a coherent and useful one? These questions are obviously interrelated.

To begin with the question of the content of the concept of "justice," it is striking how unclear this concept is in ordinary language and to what extent conceptions of justice differ from one context to another and in different human societies at different times. Thus at the beginning of one of the standard treatises of Roman law, the codification made for the emperor Justinian[33]—one of the most influential texts in European history—we find that the very first sentence gives us a definition of "justice": "iustitia est constans et perpetua voluntas ius suum cuique tribuens." That is, justice is "the constant and unflagging will to give to each person what is due to him" (or perhaps: "what he is entitled to").[34] This notion of *ius suum* is one of the kernels in Roman law from which eventually the full-blown concept of a subjective right will develop. For a modern philosophical sensibility this definition seems slightly eccentric, because it seems focused on the virtue of justice as a property of a human agent (who has a "will") rather than on the systematic properties of a social system, and obviously this formula is utterly empty and unenlightening until one can say what *ius suum* (what he is entitled to) actually means. *Ius suum* turns out to be a wide variety of different, disparate things. In fact, the warm glow of pseudofamiliarity this formula might initially generate in us will immediately be dispelled when we go on to read the very next sections of the standard text on Roman law, which inform us that a fundamental and essential step in understanding justice is to discriminate between kinds of people because different people (adult free men, women who are minors, slaves) are entitled to radically different things: Roman citizens have certain entitlements; resident aliens have a different set of entitlements; some humans, slaves, are entitled to nothing at all. To be just is to treat others according to their respective entitlements. The ideally just man owes slaves simply nothing. A gentleman will not mistreat a slave, but this is a question of decorum, *humanitas*, or the aesthetic self-stylisation of the aristocratic life, not a question of justice. A gentleman in the ancient world would in any case have held himself to a standard different from the one he applied to other people or the one other people used among themselves.[35] Justice would have been no more than a minor consideration for him. The Roman legal code conceptualised with firm and unwavering clarity the almost universally shared "intuition" that to treat a slave as if he or she had *any* entitlements would be a gross violation of the basic principles of justice.

Another way to develop the intuition that lies behind the Roman formula *suum ius cuique tribuendum* is to detach *ius* from its connection to a particular positive legal system. Certain things might be thought to be "due" to me independently of whether or not they were recognised by the legal code that happened to be enforced. Thus I might try to appeal to such notions as "desert" or "merit." It is just that the runner who crosses the finishing line first be declared "winner" because he or she has "deserved" to win, even if the race is an informal one and the result has no legal standing. I merely mention here that notions of desert and merit are at least as variable as legal systems, and that many of these notions seem to have a kind of inbuilt bias toward inequality: the "merit" that "ought to be rewarded" is being or doing better than others; the sick "deserve" more medical attention because they are less functional or "more needy" than the healthy.

If Roman law seems too unreflective a point to start from, perhaps we would do better to turn to Aristotle. We all remember his distinction in book 5 of *The Nicomachean Ethics* that invokes one sense of "justice" in which we use the term simply to designate the presence of all the virtues or excellences together in general (ἀρετὴ τελεία *EN* 1129b26, or ὁλὴ ἀρετὴ *EN* 1130a9, or even κρατίστη τῶν ἀρετῶν δοκεῖ εἶναι ἡ δικαιοσύνη *EN* 1129b27–8, or "ἐν δικαιοσύνηι συλλήβδην πᾶσ᾽ ἀρετὴ ἐνι *EN* 1129b 29–30). Let us call this the "general" concept of justice. Aristotle then distinguishes *another* sense in which "justice" designates not the whole of virtue, but a particular virtue, which is merely one part of excellence (ἡ ἐν μέρει ἀρετῆς δικαιοσύνη *EN* 1130a14). Aristotle's own discussion of the particular virtue of "justice" is very complex, much too complicated for treatment here, but for present purposes one can isolate a strand in it that connects "justice" with "the equal" rather than the "unequal," especially when distribution of goods is at issue.[36] The idea here is presumably that "other things beings equal"—an extremely important qualification—a just distribution of goods that are up for division among a number of different people is one that gives to each an equal share. "Equal," however, in what respect?

Equality

This brings us to the notion of "equality," which is perhaps part of the motivation behind various specific attempts to promote the status of "justice" in politics. Many have found it tempting to follow the French Revolutionaries in counting *Égalité* as one of the cardinal political virtues. No one, to be sure, who wished to follow the lead of Marx and Engels even approximately could take this line, because both of them had been very firm and explicit antiegalitarians, or, rather, they had held that abstract equality as a social ideal was philosophically incoherent, and whether concrete equality in some respect was or was not desirable in some particular circumstances was always an open question. Their reflections on equality repay closer consideration.

The best way to begin here is with a general philosophical remark about identity and difference, which becomes clear if one thinks of the practice of counting. It makes no sense to speak of "counting how many things there are in this room" *tout court*, unless you antecedently specify what counts as a "thing." Are the cup and saucer "one" thing or two? Is the top of the teapot a distinct object that should be counted separately? How about the built-in sieve? Similarly, it makes no sense to speak of two "things" or states of affairs that are "equal" or "unequal," unless one specifies the dimension along which they are being compared. If two things are "equal," they will be equal *in some respect*; if they really are two distinct things at all, they will be *unequal* in other respects. If two things really were equal in *every* respect (including their history and spatiotemporal position), they would be indistinguishable, and thus by a principle that philosophers call "Leibniz's principle of identity of indiscernibles," they would, then, not be two different, but *equal*, things; rather, they would be *the very same thing*. One may say of some given object that it is "self-identical" or "equal to itself" if one wishes, but there does not seem to be much political point in doing that. The very idea of total, perfect, and complete egalitarianism can't be a social ideal of any significance because it is literally incoherent. A society is a group of distinct persons, and if it is to survive for any amount of time, it must reproduce itself, so that some of its members will not be equal to other members by virtue of being younger. The only way to attain complete equality would be to eliminate the distinctness between persons, and then there would no longer be a "society."

The concepts of "equal" and "unequal," then, are correlative to each other, and whether you describe two concrete things as "equal" (to each other) or "unequal" is always relative and depends completely on the choice of the dimension along which the comparison is made. As Marx emphasises most vividly in his discussion of this topic,[37] any attempt to make two people "more equal" along one dimension will necessarily make them more unequal along another. Marx's examples are these: If you give two people equal pay for an equal number of hours of work, you will be giving *more* total pay to the one who can work longer hours. If you give equal daily pay to each worker, by doing that you will give a single worker with no dependents more disposable income than a worker who has to support four children. These are individual examples, but Marx thinks they illustrate an absolutely general point. Because of the very nature of the concepts of equality and inequality, no *net gain* in (abstract) equality is ever attainable. In the end all one will do is move the inequality around from one dimension to another. So any reasonable discussion must shift from treating "equality" in the abstract to discussion of the various dimensions along which more equality is thought to be socially desirable, and this discussion will be a sensible one only if it includes a recognition that any increase in equality along dimension A will necessarily be accompanied by an increase in inequality along dimension B. In many cases, we think this is a reasonable trade-off to make, but that has much less to do with equality per se than with the particular characteristics of dimensions A and B.

Marx and Engels were as clear as they could possibly have been about this general point. When they turn from the abstract philosophical point to a discussion of politics, they show equally little sympathy for demands for "equality," describing the general demand for abstract equality either as a "one-sided, French" error—a confusion in which the desirability of some specific form of equality in some specified dimension was incorrectly taken to be an argument for general equality[38]—or as an expression of "envy."[39] One might criticise a particular *form* of inequality, for instance, the inequality-before-the-law of nobles, clergy, and Third Estate during the ancien régime, but this would be because of some specific drawback of this kind of juridical practice in the specified historical circumstances, not because there was anything inherently objectionable about legally recognised or even legally created human inequality. Much legally created inequality, after all, has great social value. Engels at the end of his life was emphatically of the opinion that "abolition of all hierarchies" was a typically anarchist demand (which for him was a criticism). Thus he would have approved of the fact that in most advanced countries a special licence is required to offer to perform surgical operations; the law, that is, creates a special category of privileged persons who may perform particular acts that are forbidden to others. Similarly, the members of a jury are given a privilege that other members of the society lack: they are empowered by the law to make a legally binding judgment on a particular case. In one sense the members of the jury are the "equals" of those not on the jury, but in another sense they are not.

Just to repeat this important point, the distribution of medical services in a modern hospital can be described, depending on the frame of reference chosen, as "equal" (all are to get, notionally, as much as they need), or "unequal" (those seriously ill get more treatment than those with minor ailments), and our ability to redescribe the situation in each of these two different ways is an indication of the uselessness of the distinction if used in the abstract. That this form of distribution is chosen tells you more about the role of health in a modern society than about the concept of "equality." There is nothing special about equality; what is objectionable is depriving people of needed medical treatment, if it is in principle available. *That* in most societies is a definite social ill, and we do not need to appeal to the notion of "equality" to see why it is an ill. It is not, then, that we proceed as follows: first we have an intuition about "equality" as the basis for political philosophy; then we observe that in this particular case equality is violated (because not everyone is getting "equal" medical care); finally, we infer that we are in the presence of a social evil that needs to be rectified. It is, rather, that there are any number of different reasons for thinking that mass death for want of medical help is a bad thing—it is virtually a paradigm of what we mean by a social ill—and we think that in *this* case the reason that so many people are dying is that those who need it are not receiving medical help, not that treatment is "unequally" distributed. It seems a serious confusion to shift the locus of human significance from such things as health, development and exercise of powers, fruitful social interaction, etc., on to what is at best a mere instrument or a contributory condition *in some circumstances*.

Fairness, Ignorance, Impartiality

For a variety of easily comprehensible reasons, however, including inherent difficulties with conceptions of justice centred on equality/inequality, discussion can shift from the abstract comparison of the absolute states in which different members of society find themselves—some have more wealth, some less; some work longer hours, some shorter; some have more children, some fewer; some are healthy, some ill—to the processes by which these states are assigned or distributed to different people. This, of course, presupposes that we think of society as a whole as a huge mechanism for distributing people into categories (wealthy, poor; healthy, ill; etc.) or alternatively for attributing goods, services, and other benefits to people. We can then study the rules or the procedure by which this distribution can be construed to take place. We sometimes call a procedure "just" if it is one in which appropriate consideration is given to "relevant" factors and no consideration is given to factors deemed irrelevant, even if the result of using the procedure is inequality of outcome. The doctor is being "fair," as we might be inclined to say, if he gives the one remaining shot of morphine to the man emerging from painful surgery, ignoring the claims of his brother, the drug addict, or of his sister, who simply wants to find out what it feels like to have an injection of morphine. The sense of what is "fair" depends to a high degree on the distinction between those factors that are considered to be "relevant" to the decision in question and those which are considered "irrelevant," and that distinction is historically highly variable and ex-tremely context-dependent. "Justice" then can come to be associated not with equality (being in an "equal" state to some specified other person or group) but with "fairness" of distribution.

There would seem, then, to be at least five very different ways to approach the concept of "justice." The first is the idea that justice is connected with the idea of giving each person (and group?) what is "due" to him, her, or them. One obvi-ous way to specify what it is that is "due" to someone is to appeal to existing legal codes, but what they will prescribe will vary enormously from one time and place to another. A second account of justice might appeal to some notion of merit or desert. The third approach is Aristotle's "general" conception, which simply identified "justice" with the sum of all the virtues and excellences. A fourth conception of justice is the idea that justice is in some way to be connected to equality of shares, resources, or outcomes. Finally there is the idea of fairness or impartiality of procedure.

One might think that Rawls's view derives some of its apparent plausibility because of a gradual slide between the various senses of "justice." People start from a vague intuition that justice as a "general" concept (in the third sense above) is extremely important for the proper functioning of a society; they then find it easy to shift from this to a particular conception that connects "justice" with fairness of procedure and (a certain kind of limited) equality. Then this notion of justice as fairness further slips over into the idea that a "fair" procedure is what would be chosen in the original position under the veil of ignorance. The final result is that people accept Rawls's formal principles of justice as giving the definition of the highest social virtue.

Rawls's view, however, seems deficient in a number of ways. First, perhaps one could make a case for the claim that "justice" had absolute priority over all other considerations, if one had in mind the "general" conception of justice, that is, the use of the term "justice" simply to refer to the "whole of excellence." Depending on how one construed "the whole of excellence," this might even be virtually a tautology. One might perfectly well wonder whether the very idea that a person or a society could instantiate "*all* the virtues and excellences" made much sense. Brachial strength may be a human excellence, especially in a professional pugilist; great dexterity in performing delicate manual operations may also be a human excellence, especially in a brain surgeon. There may, however, be no human individual who combines these two properties at the highest level. Discipline and good order may be excellences of a human society; spontaneity, noncoerciveness, and tolerance may also be excellences. It may, however, be no more than a pious wish, an infantile fantasy, or an ideological delusion to think that all of these properties could even in principle be maximally instantiated in the same society at the same time.[40] Whatever one might think of the coherence of trying to understand justice as "the whole of excellence," Rawls himself specifically claims that one specific kind or conception of justice has primacy: justice-as-fairness. This is an exceedingly peculiar view. Is there, however, any reason whatever to think that fairness, however construed (or "equality" in an abstract sense), has "*uncompromising*" priority over all other political and moral values: survival, security, agency, transparency, efficiency, self-esteem? Does fairness take priority no matter what? Is "fairness" clearly more important than the satisfaction of genuinely vital human interests? *Fiat justitia, ruat caelum* may be a well-known ancient tag, but it is balanced by any number of other equally pithy reminders of the highly limited range of the virtues of justice (*Inter arma silent leges*; *Salus populi suprema lex esto*; *Necessitas non habet legem*). This is perfectly clear in emergency situations: in situations of this kind most people think fairness a low priority. What is an emergency situation and who decides when one has arisen? Is it an emergency if I see the other members of my society on the point of instituting a practice that I think I *know* will have the unavoidable result of corrupting their immortal souls and damning them to eternal perdition? If my linguistic and cultural group is about to go out of existence? If the other members of my society are about to scapegoat the members of an innocent, or even a not-so-innocent, minority? (Or is that an "emergency" only for the members of the minority?) Are we really "intuitively convinced" that we ought to risk our very survival if that is the price we must pay for small violations of fairness? Isn't it more important in a famine to save the lives of as many as possible rather than to ensure that the distribution is "fair"? The same would seem to hold for situations of great affluence: if everyone has more than enough nourishing, palatable food to eat, do we care about distribution (fair or not) at all? Even in the wide range of cases that are characterised neither by urgent necessity nor by great affluence, why should it be thought unreasonable to prefer great gains in efficiency or democratic control of society or human dignity at the price of small systematic deviations from fairness? Aren't all of the above political questions? We are all familiar with individual cases in which we think humanity, decency, and charity ought to trump fairness. Should pregnant women who commit crimes be incarcerated on the same ("fair") terms as men, to take a topic that has recently been the object of some discussion in Britain? Is "uncompromising" fairness always self-evidently the right standard to use when dealing with young people? Members of despised minorities? These cases tend to be rather underexplored in the existing philosophical literature because they are practically impossible to describe in a way that both has the stylistic neutrality expected in academic discourse, and yet brings out the immediate responses many people have without giving the impression of prejudging them. However, to the extent to which we have genuinely intuitive views at all, it seems to me that there is nothing special about fairness, except in certain rather well defined contexts. It is a value that we think should play *an* important role in society, but what exact role it should play depends on circumstances; it is not thought automatically to trump all other values.

It is often unclear to what exact audience Rawls takes his theory to be directed. To whom is the "we" supposed to refer in Rawls's claim that "we" have the intuitive conviction of the absolute primacy of justice? Does "we" mean "all empirical human beings"? Then the claim that "we" think justice has priority is certainly simply false. Does "we" in a Kantian mode purport to refer to "all rational creatures" (perhaps with the addition "to the extent to which they reflect fully, carefully, and honestly on their own intuitions in optimal circumstances")? To believe that Rawls's claim about "our" intuitions concerning the priority of justice is true in this sense is to subscribe to an extremely strong, and highly implausible—that is to say, almost certainly false— thesis about the universal structures of human rationality. Sometimes Rawls's "we" seems to refer to a significantly narrower group than all humans or all rational creatures, as when he speaks of addressing his "fellow-citizens," i.e., all those who hold U.S. citizenship. If this is the case, then Rawls's theory would have value to those who are not U.S. citizens either as a rhapsodic description of a possible object of aspiration or as an object of documentary study, revealing the idiosyncrasies of a particular, albeit powerful, contemporary population. There is nothing inherently objectionable about an appeal addressed to a particular group of people, and connected with their peculiar concerns, values, and beliefs, especially a group of which one is oneself an active member, provided it is factually correct and does not overstate the advantages of its proposals while understating their drawbacks, and provided it does not present itself as something more than it is—that is, does not give itself the allure of being of universal relevance to all rational creatures. The noncognitive, potentially aspirational aspect of Rawls's view can be brought out particularly clearly if one takes "we" to refer to those who live in societies "sufficiently like [the United States]" to identify with its specific "liberal" social and political order, and who wish to institutionalise this form of liberalism in a more consistent way. How close is "close enough"?

Another way to put it is that "our intuitions," "choice under the veil of ignorance," "the original position," etc., are best understood as having a structure like that of some of the (failed) "conceptual innovations" discussed in Part I. It is a proposed innovation the success or failure of which is still an open question. These Rawlsian structures might be thought of as imaginative constructs that have not primarily an analytic or cognitive function, but persuasive and transformational power. It isn't, of course, that "we" antecedently have a fixed intuition that justice is prior to all other social and political virtues If, however, the Rawlsian theory is overall sufficiently attractive and backed by sufficient real power and sufficient social prestige, if enough people fall under the spell of becoming like the idealised agents whom Rawls's theory portrays, perhaps Rawls's doctrines will come to structure more and more people's "intuitions." If Rawlsianism were adopted by the IMF and the IMF had enough power, perhaps, it could remake the world so that almost everyone at least aspirationally identified with Rawls's "we." That would still not make Rawls's theory true. And what about those of us who might continue to dissent from Rawls's intuitions and who find his various ideals unappealing or actively repellent?

What agents would choose in certain well-defined conditions of ignorance (in the "original position") is, for Rawls, an important criterion for determining which conception of "justice" is normatively acceptable. Why should we agree that choice under conditions of ignorance is a good criterion for deciding what kind of society we would wish to have? William Morris in the late nineteenth century claimed to prefer a society of more or less equal grinding poverty for all (e.g., the society he directly experienced in Iceland) to Britain with its extreme discrepancies of wealth and welfare, even though the least well-off in Britain were in absolute terms better off than the peasants and fishermen of Iceland.[41] This choice seems to have been based not on any absolute preference for equality (or on a commitment to any conception of fairness), but on a belief about the specific social (and other) evils that flowed from the ways in which extreme wealth could be used in an industrial capitalist society.[42] Would *no one* in the original position entertain views like these? Is Morris's vote simply to be discounted? On what grounds? The "veil of ignorance" is artificially defined so as to allow certain bits of knowledge "in" and to exclude other bits. No doubt it would be possible to rig the veil of ignorance so that it blanks out knowledge of the particular experiences Morris had and the theories he developed, and renders them inaccessible in the original position, but one would then have to be convinced that this was not simply a case of modifying the conditions of the thought experiment and the procedure until one got the result one antecedently wanted.

The veil of ignorance, that is, seems likely to do both too much and too little. Too much in cases like that of William Morris—it deprives him of a bit of knowledge that he thinks is relevant, or, rather, that he thinks is *the most* relevant piece of information one can have in trying to make a reasonable decision about what kind of society one wants. Too little in the case of deeply rooted forms of oppression or ideological delusion. Think, for instance, of people in a traditionalist society in which there is broad agreement on a certain division of social roles with associated benefits and disadvantages. It has been argued that very often some groups in such societies (such as women) accept their exclusion from certain benefits because they have internalised an image of themselves as unworthy, or have developed "low aspirations." In such a society it is not useful to tell women to "imagine you don't know whether you are a woman or a man in this society," because merely *trying to imagine* one were not subject to deforming pressures that shape one's beliefs and values in a particular way, e.g., in the direction of low aspirations, will not actually do away with or root out these entrenched prejudices. To put it bluntly, women who have internalised low aspirations might well still be willing to endorse in the original position a regime that differentially benefits men. This should not be surprising; it is what is meant by saying that the members of a certain social group have genuinely internalised low aspirations. If the basic assumption of the theory of ideology is at all tenable, namely, that the general power relations embodied in our social structures can exert a distorting influence on the formation of our beliefs and preferences without our being aware of it, then we are definitely not going to put that kind of influence out of action by asking the agents in the society to *imagine* that they didn't know their position. To think otherwise is to believe in magic: imagine you are "impartial" and you will be. In fact, doing that will be more likely to reinforce the power of these entrenched prejudices because it will explicitly present them as universal, warranted by reason, etc.

Although the early Rawls was chosen as an example of the strong Kantian strand in contemporary political philosophy, if one looks at this early work in the context of the whole of Rawls's output, Rawlsian political philosophy, as it developed, seems to have stronger similarities with Hegel than with Kant. At the end of the last book he published, *The Law of Peoples*, Rawls sets out the task of "reconciling" members of "liberal democratic" societies to their social order, and interprets his own previous work as contributing to that enterprise.[43] Hegel tried to "reconcile" Prussians in the early 1820s with the Prussian state by showing that, although that state needed some far-reaching reforms, it was nevertheless fundamentally "rational" and conformed to all the intuitive demands for moral acceptability that its members might impose on it.[44] Similarly, Rawls's work was an attempt to reconcile Americans to an idealised version of their own social order at the end of the twentieth century. The religious roots of this project are rather clear, but a full account of the ideological character of Rawls's philosophy would have to analyse in detail the political consequences of the particular way in which Rawls carried the project out.[45]

Power

That brings us to the most serious general line of criticism of Rawls as a political philosopher. If one looks at the body of his work against the background of the general approach I sketched earlier in this book, one is immediately struck by the complete absence in it of any discussion of what I have described above as the basic issues of politics. The topic of "power," in particular, is simply one he never explicitly discusses at all.[46] If one thinks that ideological conceptions are an important feature of modern societies, and that the analysis of ideologies will therefore have to be an integral component of any contemporary political philosophy, Rawls's view is seriously deficient, because it does not thematise power. The idea that seems to be presupposed by the doctrine of the veil of ignorance—namely, that one can in some way get a better grasp or understanding of the power relations in society and how they work by covering them up, ignoring them, or simply wishing them away—seems very naïve. To the extent, then, to which Rawls draws attention *away* from the phenomenon of power and the way in which it influences our lives and the way we see the world, his theory is itself ideological. To think that an appropriate point of departure for understanding the political world is *our* intuitions of what is "just," *without* reflecting on where those intuitions come from, how they are maintained, and what interests they might serve, seems to exclude from the beginning the very possibility that these intuitions might themselves be "ideological." Even, however, if one wished to have no truck with any concept of "ideology," one might find it highly peculiar to present what is supposed to be a reasonably full overview of any social and political system without giving any explicit attention to the relations of power that exist in that system, and the way power can influence thought, feeling, and valuation.

To repeat, a weakness of approaches to politics through "intuitions" is that such intuitions present themselves at any given time as if they were firmly fixed, deeply rooted in the bedrock of human nature, and utterly unchanging, although even a minimal amount of historical (or ethnological) research reveals that many of the most politically significant of these intuitions are in fact highly variable and change in ways that seem to some extent to reflect other social changes. It was at one time—for long periods of Western history—the very epitome of justice that one *not* treat all men as equal (and in particular that one *not* treat a free man like a slave or a slave like a free man). Even if we were to admit something that is by no means obvious, namely, that the "intuitions" of early twenty-first-century inhabitants of highly developed capitalist societies have some kind of canonical status as modes of access to politics or even as the starting point for understanding politics, it is not at all clear that these intuitions would support Rawls's claims about the absolute priority of justice (or equality or fairness). Do "we" really all believe that giving people with vastly different powers and resources abstractly "equal" rights (and duties and "opportunities") and abstractly "fair" conditions of interaction will *in itself* necessarily create a situation that one could reasonably judge to be in any special way evaluatively attractive? Experience shows that imposing "equal" conditions of bilateral trade on a country with a large strong economy and a country with a small, weak, or underdeveloped economy has, under modern conditions, the actual effect of impoverishing the latter and subordinating it to the needs of the former. Without some account of relative powers, imposing one law for the vulture and the lamb can easily mean death for all the lambs.[47]

Similar considerations apply to the notion of "fairness." No boxing match would be considered "fair" that pitted a child against an adult, even if all the procedural rules were followed to the letter. In fact, most real judgments of what is "fair" have built into themselves some judgment of the relative powers of the persons and groups involved in the interaction, and try to correct for these. Adults racing against children may give the children a head start. It is a bad idea to base one's political philosophy on our given intuitions, but even if one held that intuitions could have some limited value, it seems that Rawls has got "our" intuitions wrong. These cases suggest that even "our" intuitions about "fairness" include a component in which one takes some account of differences in power. One cannot do that if one has a theory in which (differential) power is invisible.

A focus on fairness without an associated account of power relations construes human life as a matter of following the rules. But is human life essentially about following pregiven rules? Is all of human society best described by any set of rules? Is politics always about adhering to and applying the rules? Do rules apply themselves? Are they not sometimes applied by people and institutions with appropriate powers? Rules also sometimes change although no one intends this, as when the phonetics of a language gradually changes over time, and sometimes they are intentionally changed, as when the euro replaces the mark and franc.

Politics is *sometimes* (at least sometimes) about finding out how to change the rules of the game, and in any case rules *without power*—the power of someone who might enforce them—are empty. Fairness may be the supreme virtue of the bureaucrat, the administrator, or the umpire, but, then, is all politics administration? Can there even be administration without power?

At this point it is important to avoid a tempting mistake. One might think that what I am proposing is really that we rehabilitate "equality" by simply respecifying it relative to the correct dimension, namely, power. We don't need "equal opportunity" or "equal justice," but "equal power." That is incorrect for reasons that should be clear from the previous discussion. There is no point in preaching "equal power" per se, because what this might mean and whether or not it is at all desirable depends completely on the situation in question. Few people would prefer a social formation in which teachers and students, surgeons and patients, people with and without drivers' licenses, have "equal power" to one in which an appropriate inequality is institutionalised.

Rawls's theory purports not merely to study one specific political concept, one among others ("justice"), but to provide the *basic framework* for approaching politics. It seems reasonable, then, to hold it to a rather high standard. If one thinks that a political theory can be a good guide to action only if it is minimally realistic, in the sense of being in cognitive contact with the real world, one will demand of a candidate theory that it actively encourage one to understand the ways in which power, interests, priorities, values, and forms of legitimation concretely interact in society. An "ideal theory" without contact to reality is, then, no guide to action. The often noted absence in Rawls of any theory about how his ideal demands are to be implemented is not a tiny mole that serves as a beauty spot to set off the radiance of the rest of the face, but the epidermal sign of a lethal tumour. In real politics, theories like that of Rawls are nonstarters, except, of course, as potential ideological interventions. A theoretical approach with no place for a theory of power is not merely deeply deficient but actively pernicious, because mystifying. This is not a criticism of some individual aspect of Rawls's theory, but a basic repudiation of his whole way of approaching the subject of political philosophy.

Conclusion

If politics should be concrete, oriented toward action, and "partisan," what particular politics do I, Raymond Geuss, advocate? This is in principle a perfectly legitimate question,[48] but one that is misplaced here. The version of "contextualism" I wish to defend is definitely not a "one-size-fits-all" view. "Eventually" or "in the final analysis" political theory and philosophy are connected to practical interventions, and one ought to be clear about these, because they can never be *assumed* to be irrelevant, but that does not mean that one must expound them explicitly in every possible discussion. There should be space for a variety of different contextually specific questions one can reasonably ask in particular contexts, and this means that it is perfectly legitimate for a particular book or essay to have a narrowly focused aim. This is especially the case for a work that has criticism as a major part of its intention.

There is a variant of the objection that I do firmly reject. That is the view that a philosopher (or theorist) must be "positive," i.e., that one may criticise some doctrine or institution only if one has a positive alternative to it to propose. This may be a good principle in certain well-defined practical situations, and certainly it is important in trying to understand politics and gauge the effectiveness of specific proposals to realise that people for perfectly comprehensible reasons are unwilling to abandon familiar, large-scale institutions and structures of action, unless they have very powerful and robust reasons for thinking there is a viable alternative that is realistically accessible to them at the moment. This may be true despite the fact that they recognise clearly the deficiencies of their institutional arrangements. On the other hand, any society has a tendency to try to mobilise human inertia in order to protect itself as much as possible from radical change, and one main way in which this can be done is through the effort to impose the requirement of "positivity" or "constructiveness" on potential critics: you can't criticise the police system, the system of labour law, the organisation of the health services, etc., unless you have a completely elaborated, positive alternative to propose. I reject this line of argument completely: to accept it is to allow the existing social formation to dictate the terms on which it can be criticised, and to allow it to impose a theoretically unwarranted burden of positive proof on any potential critic. It is perfectly legitimate, I think, to criticise "Kantian liberalism" on any number of grounds, and one does not need a fully developed theory of an alternative political philosophy or of an alternative social formation in order to do that.[49] In extremis, Brecht is perfectly right: "Nothing but *ad hominem* abuse; that's better than nothing" ("Nichts als Beschimpfungen, das ist mehr als nichts").[50]

If one wanted to put my point in a very general way, something that, given my contextualist predilections, I am not keen to do, one might say that modern politics is importantly about power, its acquisition, distribution, and use.

There is no reason to be narrow-minded about what counts as power, restricting it to armies and industrial plants, but still politics is not exclusively or in the first instance about our individual or collective moral intuitions. Rather than following Rawls's injunction (If you want to think about politics, think about our intuitions about justice), I am suggesting a different injunction: If you want to think about politics, think first about power. I make no claims to the effect that "power" is a necessary object of universal interest in the sense in which, according to Rawls, "justice" was supposed to be. It is merely an empirically general fact about societies we know (those that have existed in Europe during the past two thousand years or so, and some others) that in them power is going to be of interest. In Foucault's terms: power is the present danger.[51] This means not that it is inherently bad—it would make no sense to claim that. Rather, it merely means that it is advisable to pay attention to it. Perhaps one day it will not be so important. Whether or not it is better for there to be "equal power" (assuming we knew what that meant) rather than "unequal power" between given individuals is a question to which no general answer can be given. It depends completely on the specific circumstances.

Politics is a craft or skill, and ought precisely *not* to be analysed, as Plato's Socrates assumes, as the mastery of a set of principles or theories. This does not imply that political agents do not use theories. Rather, part of their skill depends on being able to choose skilfully which models of reality to use in a certain context, and to take account of ways in which various theories are limited and ways in which they are useful or fail. The successful exercise of this skill is often called "political judgment." Thus, to give one recent example of the exercise of such judgment, many of the supporters of the Second Gulf War argued that at the end of World War II the United States was able successfully to impose a democratic political form upon Germany and Japan once they were defeated militarily, and both of these countries eventually prospered under this externally imposed regime; the same, they argued, could be true in Iraq. Some opponents of the war argued that the relevant analogy was Vietnam: as soon as Saddam Hussein was toppled, the various religious and ethnic groups who constituted the population of Iraq would begin fighting, and the United States would find itself in the middle of a civil war that it would not begin to understand and from which it would find it impossible to extract itself without heavy loss of life and international standing. Beforehand, it was perhaps not obvious which analogy would turn out to be the right one. In retrospect, given the outcome of the invasion of Iraq,[52] it should now be clear that the first of these two arguments was mistaken, but even now it is an open question in *which* particular respects the analogy did not hold. Political judgment means, among other things, the ability to determine which analogies are useful, which theories abstract from crucial aspects of the situation. No further theory will help you avoid the need to judge.

As I stated at the beginning of this book, much contemporary political philosophy in the Western world is overwhelmingly neo-Kantian in its inspiration. A "neo-Kantian," of course, need not endorse all the specific claims made by the historical philosopher Immanuel Kant. The early twentieth-century philosopher C. I. Lewis described himself as a Kantian who thought every one of the specific characteristic epistemological and metaphysical theses the historical

Kant actually defended was incorrect, and Lukács said that to be a Marxist was to have a certain method—to look at society as a historically constituted dialectical "totality"—so that one could in principle be an orthodox Marxist who rejected every one of Marx's own specific beliefs.[53] Similarly, one might reasonably call oneself a "neo-Leninist" without thereby being committed to every particular view or theory the historical Vladimir Ilyich Ulyanov held. In my view, if political philosophy wishes to be at all connected with a serious understanding of politics, and thus to become an effective source of orientation or a guide to action, it needs to return from the present reactionary forms of neo-Kantianism to something like the "realist" view, or, to put it slightly differently, to neo-Leninism.

Nothing in this book should be taken to imply that no one should ever allow normative considerations of any kind to play any role whatever in deciding how to act politically. After all, even "efficiency" is a kind of normative concept. Equally I have given no reason to think that all *moral* considerations must be absolutely excluded from politics. Individuals or groups can cultivate their ethical intuitions and exercise their capacities for moral approval or disapproval *ad libitum*, as long as they do not confuse that with attaining any understanding whatever of the world in which they live, or think that their (clarified) moral intuitions have some special standing as completely adequate guides to political action. Finally, I have no objection to the view that "justice" (in whatever sense) or certain forms of "equality" are political desiderata (among others), as long as this is not construed as an abstract, blanket commitment that overrides all others, and provided particular reasons are given for thinking equality is desirable in some concrete situation. Considerations of fairness, equality, justice, and other virtues might well have a perfectly dignified, if subordinate, place in various administrative decisions. What I do object to is the claim that they define politics. One result of taking seriously the reflections presented in this book would be that we would give up approaching politics in general by trying, necessarily unsuccessfully, to blank out history, and we would also give up focusing our thinking exclusively on the set of highly peculiar and historically contingent intuitions about "justice" that we happen to find in one contemporary society.

One of the main affects motivating those who cling to the ethics-first view is, I think, the fear that if we don't keep talking about morality in the abstract, we will lose the motivation to act in ways that require a certain amount of self-discipline, self-restraint, or self-sacrifice. This fear is ungrounded. Evaluative discourse is a part of the very texture of our lives, and we are not in any danger of losing our grip on it. Perhaps all humans have potential access to—or perhaps one should, rather, say "are subject to"—experiences in which the very distinctions between good and bad, useful and useless, attractive and repulsive, blur or drop away completely.[54] Perhaps it represents a particularly high form of the religious life or poetic consciousness, not merely to be occasionally and inexplicably felled by such experiences, but systematically to *unlearn* the distinction between attractive and repulsive, good and bad, horrible and sublime; this, however, is an exhausting task of which few humans have seemed capable.[55] Socially organised humans for as long as we have been able to study them have shown themselves by and large to have had a completely robust hold on the general idea that the world could be evaluatively assessed, although, of course, they disagreed radically on the form that assessment should take and the terms in which it should be couched. Specifically moralising discourse is a lubricant for particular kinds of social interactions. Its effectiveness has been variable, but certainly less than often advertised. Two thousand (and more) years of moral preaching have not seemed to provide much evidence that this is an effective way to improve human behaviour, and training children properly self-evidently does not require having the correct "ideal theory." "Morality" in post-Christian Europe is a huge intellectual and psychological apparatus that aims to simplify our world by dividing human actions into two dichotomous categories: good and evil, with nothing in between. It has little to tell us about real politics.

Notes

1. The historical figure whose work seems to me most enlighten-
ing about the issues treated in this paragraph is Montaigne.
See especially his essays "Du repentir" and "De l'experience."
Montaigne, *Essais* (Flammarion, 1979), 3:20–33, 275–328.

2. Karl Marx, *Grundrisse der Kritik der politischen Ökonomie*
(Dietz, 1953), p. 13.

3. See Wolfgang Schivelbusch, *Die Kultur der Niederlage* (Alexander Fest Verlag, 2001), and John Dower, *Embracing Defeat:
Japan in the Aftermath of World War II* (Penguin, 1999).

4. Contra Habermas. See his *Theorie des kommunikativen Handelns*, 2 vols. (Suhrkamp, 1981), and also his *Zur Rekonstruktion des historischen Materialismus* (Suhrkamp, 1976).

5. Immanuel Kant, *Grundlegung zur Metaphysik der Sitten*
(Hartknoch, 1785), pp. 20–21.

6. Trotsky seems to have held that one could say if one wished
that there were "elementary moral precepts" that were "indispensable for the existence of every collective body," but
that they were also so vacuous and of such "indeterminate
character" that they could have little actual bearing on deciding how to act. See Leon Trotsky and John Dewey, *Their Morals and Ours* (Pathfinder Press, 1973), pp. 21–22. The young
Lukács gives a decidedly more existentialist account of ethics
in the papers from 1918–20 collected in his *Ethik und Taktik*
(Luchterhand, 1975).

7. See also my "Was ist ein politiches Urteil? " *Deutsche Zeitschrift für Philosophie* 55 (summer 2007).

8. Feodor Dostoyevsky, *Notes from Underground*, trans. Constance Garnett (Dell, 1960); see also Michel Foucault, "Le nuage et la poussière," in *L'Impossible prison* (Seuil, 1980).

9. On the difference between "questions" (or "problems") and "truths," see Max Weber, "Die 'Objektivität' sozialwissenschaftlicher und sozialpolitischer Erkenntnis," in his *Gesammelte Aufsätze zur Wissenschaftstheorie* (Mohr, 1974), pp. 146–214.

10. Marx, *Grundrisse*, pp. 5–31.

11. Wilhelm von Humboldt, *Ideen zu einem Versuch die Grenzen der Wirksamkeit des Staates zu bestimmen* (1795; Reclam, 1967).

12. See also Michel Foucault, *Surveiller et punir* (Gallimard, 1975), Steven Lukes, *Power: A Radical View* (Macmillan, 1974), and the essays in *Power*, ed. S. Lukes (New York University Press, 1986).

13. See Nadezhda Mandelstamm's *Hope against Hope: A Memoir*, trans. Max Hayward (Atheneum, 1970).

14. See *Materialism and Empirio-criticism* (Foreign Languages Press, 1972).

15. See ibid., chapter 6.

16. See Plato, *Phaidros* 244–57, esp. 252–54.

17. In the ancient world the notion of 'καιρός' is discussed in greatest detail by medical writers and military theorists. See Polybios 9.12–16 and the Hippokratic corpus.

18. Habermas, *Theorie des kommunikativen Handelns* and *Zur Rekonstruktion des historischen Materialismus*. See also Günter Dux, *Die Logik der Weltbilder* (Suhrkamp, 1982).

19. See Friedrich Nietzsche, *Zur Genealogie der Moral*, Zweite Abhandlung §8, in *Nietzsches Werke: Kritische Studien-Ausgabe*, ed. Giorgio Colli and Mazzino Montinari (de Gruyter, 1967), 5:306.

20. Lenin, *Materialism and Empirio-criticism*.

21. See Martin Heidegger, "Die Zeit des Weltbildes," in *Holzwege* (Klostermann, 1963), pp. 69–105.
22. Emile Durkheim, *Le suicide* (Presses Universitaires de France, 1930).
23. See Quentin Skinner, "The State," in *Political Innovation and Conceptual Change*, ed. T. Ball, J. Farr, and R. Hanson (Cambridge University Press, 1989), pp. 90–113, and Max Weber, *Politik als Beruf* (Duncker und Humblot, 1977), pp. 7–14.
24. See John Dunn, *Setting the People Free* (Grove Atlantic, 2005).
25. Max Weber, *Die protestantische Ethik und der Geist des Kapitalismus*, in *Gesammelte Aufsätze zur Religionssoziologie* (Mohr, 1920), vol. 1.
26. See the excellent *On Voluntary Servitude* by Michael Rosen (Polity Press, 1996).
27. Jacques Attali in a recent book (*Une brève histoire de l'avenir* [Fayard, 2006]) uses the illuminating expression "canalisation des desires vers leur expression marchande" (e.g., p. 164) to describe one of the tendencies of the "long history" of our economic formation.
28. See Richard Dragger, "Rights," in *Political Innovation and Conceptual Change*, ed. T. Ball, J. Farr, and R. Hanson (Cambridge University Press, 1989).
29. Robert Nozick, *Anarchy, State, and Utopia* (Basic Books, 1974).
30. For an instance of the political theory very firmly based on a doctrine of "rights" that, however, comes to markedly different conclusions from those reached by Nozick, see Johann Gottlieb Fichte, *Der geschlossene Handelsstaat* (1800), in *Fichtes Werke*, ed. I. H. Fichte (de Gruyter, 1971), 3:400–402, 440–47.
31. See Peter Garnsey, *Thinking about Property: From Antiquity to the Age of Revolution* (Cambridge University Press, 2008).
32. Rawls continued to publish prolifically after 1971, and there are complex issues of interpretation about the extent to which the later work can be seen as a continuation of the theory

outlined in *A Theory of Justice* and the extent to which later
writings represent revisions of the early position. "Rawls" in
the following means the author of *A Theory of Justice*.

33. *Imperatoris Iustiniani Institutes*, ed. J. B. Moyle (Oxford University Press, 1883).

34. The modern editor of the edition I am using, Moyle, points to parallel discussions in Simonides (as cited in Plato, *Republic*, bk. 1), and Cicero, *de finibis* 5.23, and *de officiis* 1.2.3.2.

35. Michel Foucault, *L'Histoire de la sexualité*, vol. 2, *L'usage des plaisirs* (Gallimard, 1984).

36. The other two strands (a) construe "justice" as the opposite of the vice πλεονεξία or (b) see "justice" as being concerned with appropriate punishment of crimes. See Aristotelis, *Ethica Nicomachea*, bk. 5.

37. *Kritik des Gothaer Programms*, in *Marx-Engels-Werke* (Dietz, 1968), vol. 19, esp. pp. 18–22.

38. Ibid.

39. *Marx-Engels-Werke*, Ergänzungsband 1, pp. 534–35.

40. The best-known recent philosophic proponent of this view, which goes back to the German Romantics, is Isaiah Berlin. See his *Four Essays on Liberty* (Oxford, 1969).

41. See William Morris, *Political Writings* (International Publishers, 1953), p. 14, and William Morris, *News from Nowhere* (Cambridge University Press, 1995).

42. See John Dunn, *The Cunning of Unreason* (Harper Collins, 2000), pp. 278–80; see also Slavoj Žižek, *How to Read Lacan* (Granta, 2006), p. 36.

43. John Rawls, *The Law of People* (Harvard, 1999), pp. 124–80.

44. G. W. Friedrich Hegel, *Grundlinien der Philosophie des Rechts*, in *Hege Werke inzwanzig Bänden* (Suhrkamp, 1970), ed. Moldenhauer and Michel, vol. 7, esp. pp. 11–28, 245–60, 406–10. See also Michael Hardimon, *Hegel's Social Philosophy: The Project of Reconciliation* (Cambridge University Press, 1994).

45. Many of the issues raised in this paragraph will be treated in more detail in Jörg Schaub's forthcoming *Gerechtigkeit als*

Versöhnung. I have profited greatly from discussions with him about the relation between Hegel and Rawls.

46. See Sheldon Wolin, *Politics and Vision*, expanded ed. (Princeton University Press, 2004), pp. 529–56.

47. Nietzsche, *Zur Genealogie der Moral*, Erste Abhandlung §13, in *Nietzsches Werke*, 5:278–79.

48. Those interested in my own political view can consult "The Politics of Managing Decline," *Theoria* 108 (December 2005).

49. The informed reader will recognise this motif from the writings of Adorno, at its most uncompromising, perhaps in "Marginalien zu Theorie und Praxis, " in *Stichworte: Kritische Modelle 2* (Suhrkamp, 1970), pp. 169–91. I think it possible to retain much of Adorno's analysis within a (revised) Leninist framework, but this is not a claim I propose to discuss in these pages.

50. Bertold Brecht, *Schriften zur Politik und Gesellschaft 1919–56* (Suhrkamp, 1974), p. 311.

51. See Michel Foucault, "À propos de la genéologie de l'éthique," in *Dits et écrits* (Gallimard, 1994), 4:386.

52. It is possible to argue that *on balance* the invasion of Iraq has been a success on its own terms if one takes its real goal to have been to ensure U.S. control of Iraqi oil.

53. Georg Lukács, *Geschichte und Klassenbewußtsein* (Luchterhand, 1968), pp. 58–59.

54. See Martin Heidegger, *Sein und Zeit* (Niemeyer, 1963), §40, pp. 184–91; see also Friedrich Nietzsche, *Die Geburt der Tragödie aus dem Geiste der Musik*, §§1–4, in *Nietzsches Werke*, 1:25–42.

55. On "poetic consciousness," see Peter Szondi, *Celan-Studien* (Suhrkamp, 1982), pp. 113–25.

Works Cited

Aristotle, Cicero, and Plato are cited from the most recent Oxford Classical Text editions. Usable bilingual editions of Polybius are available in Budé (Greek/French) and Loeb (Greek/English).

Adorno, Theodor. "Marginalien zu Theorie und Praxis." In his *Stichworte Kritische Modelle 2*. Suhrkamp, 1970.

Attali, Jacques. *Une brève histoire de l'avenir*. Fayard, 2006.

Berlin, Isaiah. *Four Essays on Liberty*. Oxford, 1969.

Brecht, Bertold. *Schriften zur Politik und Gesellschaft 1919–56*. Suhrkamp, 1974.

Dostoievsky, Feodor. *Notes from Underground*. Translated by Constance Garnett. Dell, 1960.

Dower, John. *Embracing Defeat: Japan in the Aftermath of World War II*. Penguin, 1999.

Dragger, Richard. "Rights." In *Political Innovation and Conceptual Change*, edited by T. Ball, J. Farr, and R. Hanson. Cambridge University Press, 1989.

Dunn, John. *The Cunning of Unreason*. Harper Collins, 2000.

———. *Setting the People Free*. Grove Atlantic, 2005.

Durkheim, Emile. *Le suicide*. Presses Universitaires de France, 1930.

Dux, Günter. *Die Logik der Weltbilder*. Suhrkamp, 1982.

Fichte, Johann Gottlieb. *Der geschlossene Handelsstaat*. 1800. In *Fichtes Werke*, edited by I. H. Fichte, vol. 3. de Gruyter, 1971.

Foucault, Michel. "À propos de la genéologie de l'éthique. " In *Dits et écrits*, vol. 4..Gallimard, 1994.

——. "Le nuage et la poussière." In *L'impossible prison.* Seuil, 1980.

——. *L'Histoire de la sexualité*. Vol. 2, *L'usage des plaisirs*. Gallimard, 1984.

Garnsey, Peter. *Thinking about Property: From Antiquity to the Age of Revolution.* Cambridge University Press, 2008.

Geuss, Raymond. "The Politics of Managing Decline." *Theoria* 108 (December 2005).

——. "Was ist ein politisches Urteil? " *Deutsche Zeitschrift für Philosophie* 55 (summer 2007).

Habermas, Jürgen. *Theorie des kommunikativen Handelns.* 2 vols. Suhrkamp, 1981.

——. *Zur Rekonstruktion des historischen materialismus.* Suhrkamp, 1976.

Hardimon, Michael. *Hegel's Social Philosophy: The Project of Reconciliation.* Cambridge University Press, 1994.

Hegel. G.F.W. *Grundlinien der Philosophie des Rechts.* In *Hegel Werke in zwanzig Bänden*, edited by Moldenhauer and Michel, vol. 7. Suhrkamp, 1970.

Heidegger, Martin. "Die Zeit des Weltbildes. " In *Holzwege.* Klostermann, 1963.

——. *Sein und Zeit.* Niemeyer, 1963.

Humboldt, Wilhelm von. *Ideen zu einem Versuch die Grenzen der Wirksamkeit des Staates zu bestimmen.* 1795. Reclam, 1967.

[Justinian.] *Imperatoris Iustiniani Institutes.* Edited by J. B. Moyle. Oxford University Press, 1883.

Kant, Immanuel. *Grundlegung zur Metaphysik der Sitten.* Hartknoch, 1785.

Lenin, V. I. *Materialism and Empirio-criticism.* Foreign Languages Press, 1972.

Lukács, Georg. *Ethik und Taktik.* Luchterhand, 1975.

——. *Geschichte und Klassenbewußtsein.* Luchterhand, 1968.

Lukes, Steven. *Power: A Radical View.* Macmillan, 1974.

——, ed. *Power.* New York University, 1986.

Mandelstamm, Nadezhda. *Hope against Hope: A Memoir*. Translated by Max Heyward. Atheneum, 1970.

Marx, Karl. *Grundrisse der Kritik der politischen Ökonomie*. Dietz, 1953.

———. *Kritik des Gothaer Programms*. In *Marx-Engels-Werke*, vol. 19. Dietz, 1972.

———. *Ökonomisch-Philosophische Manuskripte (1844)*. In *Marx-Engels-Werke*, Ergänzungsband 1. Dietz, 1968.

Montaigne, Michel. *Essais*. Flammarion, 1979.

Morris, William. *News from Nowhere*. Cambridge University Press, 1995.

———. *Political Writings*. International Publishers, 1953.

Nietzsche, Friedrich. *Die Geburt der Tragödie aus dem Geiste der Musik*. In *Nietzsches Werke: Kritische Studien-Ausgabe*, edited by Giorgio Colli and Mazzino Montinari, vol. 1. de Gruyter, 1967.

———. *Zur Genealogie der Moral*. In *Nietzsches Werke: Kritische Studien-Ausgabe*, edited by Giorgio Colli and Mazzino Montinari, vol 5. de Gruyter, 1967.

Nozick, Robert. *Anarchy, State, and Utopia*. Basic Books, 1974.

Rawls, John. *The Law of People*. Harvard University Press, 1999.

———. *A Theory of Justice*. Harvard University Press, 1971.

Rosen, Michael. *On Voluntary Servitude*, Polity Press, 1996.

Schaub, Jörg. *Gerechtigkeit als Versöhnung*. Forthcoming, 2008.

Schivelbusch, Wolfgang. *Die Kultur der Niederlage*. Alexander Fest Verlag, 2001.

Skinner, Quentin. "The State." In *Political Innovation and Conceptual Change*, edited by T. Ball, J. Farr, and R. Hanson. Cambridge University Press, 1989.

Szondi, P. *Celan-Studien*. Suhrkamp, 1982.

Trotsky, Leon (and John Dewey). *Their Morals and Ours*. Pathfinder Press, 1973.

Weber, Max. "Die 'Objektivität' sozialwissenschaftlicher und sozialpolitischer Erkenntnis." In his *Gesammelte Aufsätze zur Wissenschaftstheorie*. Mohr, 1974.

———. *Politik als Beruf.* Duncker und Humblot, 1977.

———. Die protestantische Ethik und der Geist des Christentums in Gesammelte Aufsätze zur Religionssoziologie. Vol. 1. Mohr, 1920.

Wolin, Sheldon. *Politics and Vision.* Expanded ed. Princeton University Press, 2004.

Žižek, Slavoj. *How to Read Lacan.* Granta, 2006.

Index

action, 1–2, 5–6, 8–16, 21–22,
  31–32, 34–35, 37–38, 40–42,
  70, 93–94, 99
administration, 93, 100
Adorno, T. W., 107n49
Afghanistan, 6
Algeria, 5
anomie, 41
Aristotle, 38, 75–76, 82
art, politics as. *See* craft
assessment. *See* values
attention, 52–53, 67, 68, 69, 90,
  97
authority, 44–45, 47

Baghdad, 23
benefit, 22, 25–26, 88
Brecht, Bertold, 96
Bush administration, 31

Cartesianism, 2–3
cat-lure, 49
Catullus, 3
Charlemagne, 35–36

Christianity, 8, 12–13, 39
context , 11, 13–14, 17, 24–25, 29,
  81, 95–97
contingency, 2, 9, 52, 67, 69,
  100
craft, politics as, 15–16, 32–33,
  97–98
criticism, 53, 55; billingsgate as
  legitimate form of, 96; non-
  constructive, 95–96

Darwinism, 4, 12
discussion, ideal, 31
disorder. *See* order
Dostoyevski, Feodor, 12
Durkheim, Emile, 41

envy, 78
equality, 72, 75–81, 87, 91–93,
  99–100
ethics, 1–3, 6–11; "ideal theory"
  of, 6–9, 93–94, 101
evaluation, 39–40
evil, concept of, 46

fairness, 72, 81–84, 91–93, 100
fallacy, genetic, 67
Fichte, J. G., 105n30
finitude of human existence,
    30, 37
force. *See* violence
Foucault, Michel, 97
Franciscans, 65
Führerprinzip, 46–47

genetic fallacy, 58
geometry, 2, 48

Habermas, J., 31, 36
Hegel, G.W.F., 89
history, 2, 6–9, 13–15, 32–33,
    35–36, 38, 47, 51–52, 59–60,
    64–72, 79, 81, 91, 100; phi-
    losophy of 32–33
Hobbes, Thomas, 21–22, 23, 49,
    50
Humboldt, Wilhelm von, 24
hunger, 4, 14

Iceland , 87
"ideal theory" of ethics. *See*
    ethics: "ideal theory" of
identity and difference, 76–80
identity of indiscernibles, 77
ideology, 50–55, 88–91, 94
illusion, 11, 16, 25, 53–55, 83, 88
imagination, 9–11, 24, 27, 42,

46, 48–49, 64–65, 67, 69–70,
    83, 86, 88–89
inconsistency of beliefs and
    desires, 3–4
indeterminacy of beliefs and
    desires, 2–3, 48, 51
individualism, 7
innovation, conceptual, 42–50,
    86
instability of belief and desire,
    4–5
interests, 3, 6, 7, 25, 43, 51–54,
    83, 90, 93
intuitions, ethical, 7–8, 59–60,
    71, 73, 74, 82, 85–86, 89,
    90–92, 97, 99–100
Iraq, 6, 31, 33, 98
Is/Ought distinction, 16–17
ius sum, 73–75

Jesus, 65
justice, 70–76, 81–87, 99–100,
    106n36
Justinian, Emperor, 73

καιρός, 31, 72, 104n17
Kant, 7–8, 48, 89, 98–99
Kantianism, 1, 7–8, 16–17,
    48–49, 85, 89, 96, 98–99
Keynes , John M., 3

law. *See* legal system; Roman
    law
learning, 5–6, 100

legal system, 59, 62–63, 65, 66, 73–75, 79, 81
legitimacy, 34–36, 93
Leibniz, 77
Lenin, V. I., 23, 25–30, 32, 33, 40, 98–99
Lewis, C. I., 98
liberalism, 24–25, 86, 89, 96
Logik der Weltbilder, 36
Lukács, G., 99, 103n6

market, free, 51–52, 54
Marx, Karl, 28, 41, 77–78, 99
Marx and Engels, 76–79
Marxism, 32–33, 36, 99
meaningfulness of life, 40–42
merit, 75, 82
metaphysical need, 40–41
Montaigne, 103n1
morality, 99–101
Morris, William, 87–88
motivation, 9, 100

Nietzsche, F., 23, 30, 32, 39, 41, 46, 49, 54
Nozick , Robert, 64, 67

order, 22–23, 46, 50, 83, 89; in the sense of "sequence," 30–31
orientation, general, 40–42
"original position," 71–73, 86–88

partisanship, 29–30, 95
Pater Patriae, 72
Paul of Tarsus, 12
phalanstère, 46–47
philosophy, political, 9–18, 21–23, 37
pope, the, 35–36
Potsdam Conference, 12
power, 4, 11, 25–28, 37, 42–43, 47, 50–54, 88–94, 96–97
priorities, 30–34, 54, 83, 85, 86, 91, 94

rationality, 3, 9, 12–13, 85, 89
Rawls, John, 70–73, 82–94, 97
Reagan, Ronald, 5
realism, 9–11, 22–23, 36, 59–60, 93–94
reconciliation, 89
religion, 41, 46, 89, 100. *See also* Christianity
respice finem, 10
rights, 59–70
Roman law, 11, 65, 73–75
rules, following, 92–93
Rumsfeld, Donald, 23

skill. *See* craft
slavery, 41, 74, 91
Social Democrats, 32
Socrates, 97
Stalin, Joseph, 12, 13

state, the (concept of), 44–47, 66

Suez, 5

Tabitha, 49

theorisation, politics of, 29

Third Way, the, 46–47, 53

timing, 31–34

tradition, 34, 88

Trotsky, L., 103n6

Truman, Harry, 12, 13

Underground Man. *See* Dostoyevski, Feodor

understanding, 37–38, 40

values, 1–4, 10, 15–17, 30, 39–40, 43, 83, 85–86, 91, 93, 100–101

"veil of ignorance," the, 71, 73, 86–88, 90

Vietnam, 5, 98

violence, 34–35

virtues, 59, 75–76, 82–83, 86, 93

vita apostolica, 65

Weber, Max, 23, 32, 34–35

Who whom?, 23–26

worldview, 40–42